The Cathedrals

The Story of
AMERICA'S BEST-LOVED GOSPEL QUARTET

The Cathedrals

from the founding members

GLEN PAYNE & GEORGE YOUNCE
with Ace Collins

ZondervanPublishingHouse
Grand Rapids, Michigan

A Division of HarperCollins*Publishers*

The Cathedrals
Copyright © 1998 by Traylor Publishing and Recording, Inc.

Requests for information should be addressed to:

Zondervan Publishing House
Grand Rapids, Michigan 49530

ISBN 0-310-20983-8

This edition printed on acid-free paper and meets the American National Standards
Institute Z39.48 standard.

Interior design by Sherri L. Hoffman

Printed in the United States of America

God has blessed me not only with the career I always wanted, but also with a beautiful wife, whom I love dearly, and along with their spouses, three of the most wonderful and beautiful children in the world. God has also graced me with a precious gift of three grandchildren. This book is dedicated to these loved ones as well as to my brother and sister, father and mother, grandparents, and all of the members of my family who helped me live my dream.

Glen

To my wife, Clara, and my children, who have made my life so good and happy, I dedicate this book with all my gratitude and love.

To my brother Brudge, who never stopped being my big brother. Thank you for always being there for me.

To all our friends and fans who have so faithfully supported and encouraged the Cathedrals down through the years. Thank you.

George

Glen and George would like to thank their friend Ace Collins for his diligence and dedication in writing this book. Thanks also to Zondervan Publishing House for believing in this project and allowing it to become a reality.

CONTENTS

PART ONE

George's Story

chapter one

CIRCLE OF LOVE

I DON'T REMEMBER what I had done, but for some reason my mother had quietly and suddenly pulled me up from our pew seat just a few rows from the front of the church and escorted me down the center aisle to the sanctuary's main door. I am sure the entire 120-member congregation observed Mom's tight grip on my hand as well as the slightly embarrassed look etched on her face; they also probably noticed my short legs scrambling as hard as they could to keep up with my mother's steady gait. My early exit couldn't have come as much of a surprise to those who were regulars at the small Carolina church. Everyone there knew that the Lord had blessed me with too much curiosity for my own good.

When I was a child, my energy level would have rivaled most raccoons. It was simply impossible to satisfy my roving eyes and bottomless curiosity when I was confined to the boundaries created by a mother, a brother, and a hand-carved wooden church pew. So, with those parameters set and my personality defined, the fact that I had been led to walk the aisle early in the service and in the wrong direction was not something that set this particular Sunday apart from dozens of others that had gone before or scores that would come after.

I knew the routine well. Once we cleared the front steps, Mom would let go of my hand and make a left turn toward a slight rise beside the brick church and head for a tall, old tree. It was in the shade of this ancient pine that I spent most Sunday mornings contentedly playing as services continued in the tiny Yadkin Baptist Church.

But that day I didn't pass my time digging in the dirt, chasing butterflies, scouting the skies for airplanes, watching worn-out

Model Ts chug down the road, or trying to see shapes in the clouds. Instead, I studied an image brought into sharp focus when framed through a glass window pane. It was the face of my father worshiping inside the church. I studied him closely, as though training a telescope on his face. I noted his profile and caught the sparkle in his left eye. There was nothing remarkable about his height, his bearing, or his appearance, but not even Babe Ruth or Flash Gordon stood as tall in my eyes.

It wasn't my father's image that held my attention for the next four minutes, however; it was his voice. From the first note, his bass voice boomed from the church floor to the rafters and even filled the surrounding woods with a strain that was so powerful and dominating that it caused a rambunctious little boy to stop everything he was doing and listen. It was as if a spell had been cast over me. I don't know if I could have moved if I had wanted to!

What a glorious sound! It set my heart to racing and my head to shaking. My mouth must have dropped open. Little did I realize then that this one moment, crystallized and preserved deep in my soul, would define my whole life. At that time my heart was swollen up with a son's pride.

I pulled my mom aside and told her that someday I was going to be a singer too, though I never dreamed that my voice would ever be as deep or as powerful as Daddy's. Even with a child's unlimited ability to dream, I never would have imagined that I would raise the rafters or cause others to say, "My, that boy can sing!" All I really knew was that I wanted to try to be like my old man. I couldn't have picked a better role model.

Long before I had decided that my father, whose name was Tom, was just about the world's greatest bass singer, I had already confirmed in my own mind that he had to be Santa Claus's twin. When I was a toddler running around in my older brothers' hand-me-down hand-me-downs, Daddy spent long, hard days working in a cotton mill. Though I didn't know it at the time, cotton had been an important part of my life since my birth on February 22, 1930. After all, cotton was what made Patterson, North Carolina, the wide spot in the road that it was. Except for our church and a few small houses, our community consisted of the cotton mill and the company store.

And without that white plant that grew in low rows up and down the road to our house, my father and his friends wouldn't have had much to sing about.

The old company store, the very heart of my family's existence, fascinated me. Inside its plain, wooden walls was the stuff that dreams are made of. If someone in the area had a need—anything from seeds for a garden, clothes for the kids, or parts for an old car—the store had it. It was the Wal-Mart of its time, stocking candy, toys, and even some books. For a child whose inventory of possessions consisted mainly of marbles, this really was the store to end all stores.

I would spend hours stealing looks into the store. The soda pop looked cold and refreshing, and the rows of candy bars beckoned to me. There were also jacks and balls and other things I thought would make my life more complete. Yet all of them were just out of my reach. We simply couldn't afford them.

A long, plank walkway ran from the store to the mill, and there I would wait, watching intently for my father to emerge from the cotton mill at the end of his shift. I was rarely alone during these times; on most days the walkway swarmed with a host of kids playing and adults swapping stories and catching up on local news.

Even though I was only three or four years old, I noted a couple of things about some of the old men who gathered around the walk. One was their fascination for clever or cute kids. The other was that they always seemed to have a penny or nickel squirreled away somewhere in their bib overalls to give to one of the children who really impressed them. Determined to capture their interest and their money, I developed a little dance to entertain them.

By hitting the wooden walk just right with my little feet, I could make enough noise to capture everyone's attention. I would swing my hips and arms, dance in circles, and even hum a little tune. Fueled by all the attention and the desire to be rewarded, I would keep up my act until one of the men reached into his pocket, pulled out an old, leather coin purse, and tossed a penny or nickel my way. Then, a smile covering my whole face, I would scramble to retrieve my first wages as a showman before it rolled between the wooden planks. Carefully sticking it in my pocket, I would thank the friendly patron of the arts and cut loose with another jig.

I soon discovered that my encore usually earned me only a bit of applause and a few laughs, but I enjoyed the attention so much that I just kept going. On most days I danced long after my audience had exhausted their resources and turned their attention to other things. That's how much I loved to perform.

Maybe my need for attention was driven by the fact that I was the youngest child in the Younce family. The oldest member of our clan, Ruby, was the only girl. Then came my three brothers, Ray, Tommy, and "Brudge." I gave Eugene that handle because I couldn't pronounce "Brother," which was what my mother had always called my youngest brother. Because I was the baby, my four older siblings spent a great deal of their spare time teasing me. They also made sure I was spoiled. When I did something cute, everyone was called in to watch. Anything but shy, I would attempt to top my last stunt in order to delight my growing audience. It usually worked, and I loved being rewarded with laughs and hugs.

At age four or five I was too young to realize how tough things were. I had heard people talk about the Depression, and I had even seen people down on their luck roaming the country and looking for work, but none of this had sunk into my young mind. My belly was filled with our garden produce, and I had a dog that followed me everywhere, a family who loved me no matter what I did, a secure place to lay my head at night, and the woods to play in during the day. I certainly didn't know that I was considered disadvantaged or poor in many people's minds, nor did it ever dawn on me that my mother would lie awake at night worrying that we didn't have money to buy medicine or to take one of us children to the doctor when we got a cough or ran a high fever. In my mind, life was about as perfect as it could be. I may not have had the Mississippi River just outside my door, but in many ways I was Huck Finn and Tom Sawyer come to life. When one is a child, there are a lot worse things than being poor and ignorant.

We lived in a frame house across a creek from the cotton mill. There, nestled among some trees, I lived my first few years of life. Looking back now, I remember our home as being a warm and wonderful place; today people would have thought we lived in abject poverty. The wooden boards that covered the outside of the house were also the inside walls. Even though we had fireplaces at each end of the house, it must have been drafty. Yet I just don't remember it that way. I do remember, however, cold nights spent under mounds of homemade quilts and waking up to the smell of Mom's homemade biscuits. I remember listening to my father telling stories or singing songs on the front porch on warm days, and I remember hearing the rain tap dancing on our old roof. Strange, considering all we lacked, that I can only remember what a romantic and wonderful life we had. Now I have become a bit too soft to trap rabbits and hunt squirrels, and I wouldn't consider going blackberry picking without spraying myself down with a can of Off, but at the time, that hard life was a good life—which brings me back to my father.

Daddy must have had a tough time working long hours in horrible conditions. One of my fondest memories of him points out just how difficult his days must have been. I had come to the conclusion that he was Santa's brother because of the way he looked when he came out of the mill. His whole face was covered with white wisps of cotton. A total lack of ventilation coupled with the heat and the noise must have made for a miserable work environment. His throat must have burned and his lungs must have ached. Yet I never heard my dad complain. Even when he worked sixty or seventy hours per week, he never lost or hid that big, warm smile when he spotted me waiting for him on the walkway.

Looking back now, I wonder how my father and his friends could have worked such long hours for so little money in a world where dreams were kept in check by the realities of a depression, nickel-a-pound cotton, and the burdens of providing for a family. How, in the midst of having so little time to rest or relax and so many responsibilities, did Dad, Mom, and all those around us keep their faith? I can still recall hearing them talk about blessings, spelling out the ways the Lord had touched their lives. Even as a child I felt firsthand the happiness and love that were a part of their lives. Finding joy in little things, they were neither jealous nor envious, but were people with a big appetite for life.

The old Yadkin Baptist Church that I was dragged out of so often still stands, and the window through which I watched my father sing still frames choir members today. The world has changed, the nation has changed—indeed, it seems like just about everything has changed except for this one thing: the truth of God's Word. And this has anchored me through the loss of family, the struggles of youth, the battles against temptation, and my personal fight to live up to the standards my father set for his children. The first time I felt God's power move my soul was when I heard my father's voice proudly singing as a witness to God's Word. His notes were clean and strong, and his faith was even stronger. In a tiny church in a place where few people go is an anchor that has held my promise for seven decades. It is the reason I am still singing my father's song.

chapter two

THE SPRING

As soon as I was old enough to play outside, all of us Younce kids took to the woods to enter a magical place that changed every day according to our chosen adventure. An old fallen tree served as the deck of a pirate ship one day, the next as a rocket on its way to Mars, and sometimes even as a mighty horse carrying us swiftly away from the Black Knight. On other days we followed animal trails for miles, pretending we were part of Daniel Boone's party. From time to time, we refought the battle for the American frontier using a broken tree branch as a rifle. It was amazing how straight and far that make-believe gun could shoot.

I immersed myself so much in my make-believe world that even my homemade hand-me-down stick horse seemed real. I petted him, talked to him, and even allowed him to stop for food and water. Still I remember that piece of wood as a fiery steed who knew a hundred tricks and could outrun every other stallion on the open range. My parents must have had a million laughs watching a little boy make so much out of something so simple. They knew, however, that during hard times a child's best friend is a vivid imagination.

Not far from our house and right in the middle of my outdoor playground flowed a spring so cool and clean that we stored our milk and butter there to keep them from spoiling. After a day's adventure, there was no better place for a thirsty boy to be. Lying down on my stomach, I would drink the sparkling water, letting it renew my energy and reach the deepest parts of my being. This hidden spot in the woods became a safe place in the midst of a life filled with the daily uncertainties of what life held for us during those Depression days.

I still remember the spring water cooling my burning forehead after I tripped and fell into the fireplace when I was only two. I probably would have died if my five-year-old brother, Brudge, hadn't pulled me out. Even so, I had burned my hands badly, and the infection that resulted brought on a high fever. Medicines were scarce then, and my mother and father must have been worried sick over my injuries. Their long and powerful prayers at my bedside and the refreshing nature of the spring itself made lasting impressions in my young life.

Besides the spring, my parents' voices were the other most comforting elements of my life. Dad couldn't stop singing, and I was sure he knew every song ever written. At church he didn't even seem to glance at a hymnal. Around the house he could sing everything from the most recent Jimmie Rogers or Carter Family release to old standards like "The Preacher and the Bear."

Though only about five-foot-eight, Daddy was a big man in my eyes. He was everything I thought I wanted to be. Perhaps if we had had money to go to the movies or to take in a major-league baseball game, I might have had other heroes. But I doubt it. Not even Gary Cooper or Babe Ruth could have competed with my dad's open arms, deep voice, and warm smile.

Ruby and my brothers felt that way too. Because Ruby was the oldest, she was essentially a second mother to her four brothers. Somehow my father had conveyed to her just how important this responsibility was. She not only watched over and cared for us, but she made sure each of us knew just how much it meant to be a Younce.

In those days a surname was more than something you wrote after your first name; it represented who you were. If you had a father like mine, who had spent his lifetime building a legacy of honesty, hard work, faith, and trust, you not only had to respect that image, but you were expected to live up to it. From the time we first began to put sentences together, Ruby made sure that each of us boys understood our obligations to our father and to our name.

My father never quit pressing on. Unlike most men of his generation, he recognized that there were times when he would have to take a chance and move on to a new position. I learned a great deal about courage from him because I saw that he wasn't scared to try new things. He didn't want to reach a point in his life when he stopped growing.

I was about five when Dad left his job with the cotton mill and took a position at a power plant in Buffalo Cove, West Virginia. I don't recall why he left the mill; it may have been because of the Depression and the decline in the cotton market, or it just may have been that he could make more money at the power plant. The thing I do remember is how much I missed him when he took his new job.

During the first five years of my life, Dad worked just down the Yatkin River from our house. But taking this new job meant that he had to leave early every Monday morning, spend the entire week at Buffalo Cove, and then return home on Fridays. For a boy who idolized his father, those long weeks without him were agony. When Dad had worked at the cotton mill, I had walked him home every afternoon and told him all about my daily adventures. A lot of times he had picked me up and carried me on his shoulders. It was a bonding experience that had brought us close together.

Now, for the first time in my life, evenings dragged by. But weekends were sweeter than ever. Every Friday, rather than spending the afternoon playing in the woods, I anxiously hung around the house. Most days found me tailing Ruby or my mother as they did their household chores. When supper time grew closer and the last rays of daylight began to disappear, I stood at the front door, practically pushing at the screen, as I listened for the strains of a Model-A Ford bumping down our road. As soon as I heard Dad's old car, I shoved open the door, flew off the porch, and raced to the spot where our lane met the dirt road. Then, just as Dad turned into the drive, I leaped on the running board and rode triumphantly into the front yard at my father's side. For almost a year this ritual was the most important part of my week.

Once Daddy was home, he and my brothers demanded that I fill him in on the previous Wednesday night's church service. I readily obliged, not knowing that they really wanted to watch me mimic our preacher. Mounting a stool, I would begin to quote Scripture and wave my arms wildly in the air, my voice starting low and then rising to a scream. As I stood in front of my small congregation, I demanded repentance and spoke about hell. Finally, with my voice trembling, I would ask if anyone had been moved to make a decision. As I concluded my version of the message my father had missed, he smiled and nodded his head, his eyes sparkling, then said something like, "Sounds like I missed a great deal, but thanks to you, son, I've been brought up to date." Satisfied that I had fulfilled my duty, I would proudly step down off the stool and head into the kitchen to reach the rest of my parishioners. Little did I know that I had put on a show for our entire family! But little did they realize that they were setting in motion a lifetime of work on a stage.

The Younce flock left our country home in 1936 when Dad received an offer to wire houses in the growing community of Lenoir. Just seven miles from where I had been born, Lenoir may as well have been seven hundred, since so few people traveled back then. I didn't have time to get homesick. Living in a city with more than ten thousand people opened up a whole new world. The sidewalks and long blocks of frame houses supplied countless adventures for me and my stick horse.

For the first time, I could take a bath indoors rather than outdoors in a washtub filled with branch water. I also had my first barbershop haircut. That man with those electric trimmers was about the scariest thing I had ever seen. I learned all the rules to kick the can, toss the rubber ball, and stickball. I also became a whiz at marbles and jacks. I wore shoes a lot more too.

Now that we had moved to the city and become civilized, my family was going in a lot of new directions. By this time Ruby had married and moved up the road, and Ray had a job and was courting a pretty, young woman from a neighboring town, so we didn't see much of either of them. Tommy, who was six years older than me, Brudge, and I were still at home.

We came together twice a day as a family. At supper Dad would tell us about work, Mom would catch us up on friends and family, and we kids would mainly just keep quiet and eat. Besides supper, the other gathering point was in the living room around the radio. I remember staring at that old Philco set as it played such shows as *The Lone Ranger*, *The Shadow*, *Inner Sanctum*, and *Superman*. In the radio's yellow dial, I could see everything that happened. Between the numbers I watched the progression of horses, villains, and heroes and their girls. Never have I seen television with as much detail and with as sharp a focus as I saw on our radio back then.

For the next few years, life pretty much revolved around my brothers, our simple games, the radio, church, and school. The last two of these interested me the least. Then World War II intruded upon our peaceful existence.

In 1940, when newscasts aired the details of Hitler's lust for Europe, I hadn't paid much attention—the war seemed like it was such a long way from North Carolina. Even when Pearl Harbor was hit on December 7, 1941, things didn't change much for me. After all, I was just a skinny, eleven-year-old kid whose major concern was not getting nailed for talking in class. War was nothing more to me than the games I had once played in the woods.

During the first year of the war, Ray married the daughter of West Jefferson's mayor and moved to the bride's hometown. Not long after they had set up house, the new couple invited me to stay for a couple of weeks. I had always thought Ray was such a neat guy. Blonde and good looking, before he was married he used to dress up on Saturday nights in a starched shirt, brown pants, and brown wing-tip shoes. With his muscular frame and rugged jaw, he looked like a movie star. As he left the house to go on a date, I always wondered, *Is that really my brother?* Besides my father, Ray was my hero. Thus, I was excited when he and his wife asked me to come see them.

West Jefferson was a new world for me. It had a lot of stores and great places to explore. My confidence riding high, I couldn't wait to get started. I was a skinny kid back then, and Ray, who was a rock of a young man, must have thought I needed some meat on my bones. The first day I spent with him, he took me to a drugstore and bought me the biggest milkshake I had ever seen. The next day, when Ray was at work, I decided to visit the store again. As I walked in the door, the man behind the counter asked if I wanted a milkshake. I nodded, and he fixed me one. When I finished, he inquired if I would like another. I assured him that I did. When I had finished the second one, I simply got up and left. I never thought about paying the man.

Later that day I strolled back into the store and the man again smiled and asked me if I wanted a milkshake. He didn't have to ask twice. This scene was repeated as many as five times a day for the next two weeks. I thought I had died and gone to heaven! I actually believed the guy had taken such a liking to me during my first visit that he was giving me the shakes. By the time I returned to our house on Cotton Mill Hill, I was not only a few pounds heavier, but a little wiser too. By then I had discovered that Ray had been so worried that I was too skinny to be a Younce that he had instructed the soda jerk to fatten me up to family standards no matter what the cost.

If I had my youth to live over again, the only thing I would change is my attitude about education. I thought school was pretty much a waste of time—until sixth grade, that is. That was when our music teacher decided to hold a singing contest and promised books to the boys with the highest and lowest voices. Determined to win the big prize, I practiced hard. It was the first time my mother had seen me motivated about school work, so she took time out to help me. On the day of the contest I even sang all the way to school. When my time came to sing, I gave my best Younce effort. I never will forget the look of pride on Mom's face when I waltzed into our home that afternoon with a book that declared me the winner. I had the highest voice in sixth grade! Even Dad was proud that his son showed promise as a tenor.

Like my father, my mother loved to sing. I guess she felt she had a lot to sing about. Though my mother's right arm lacked a normal range of motion and appeared shorter than her other arm due to a childhood accident, she never let that handicap hold her back, and she refused to become sour or withdrawn. Instead, she worked around the problem to become an expert seamstress, cook, and, when needed, a member of my pitch and catch team. Long on energy and patience, Mom was an optimistic, eternally happy lady. Dressed in print dresses that she made out of flour sacks, she always found the sunny side of everything. Her outlook may have been the reason I felt so happy and carefree. As long as Mom was in charge, I knew nothing bad was ever going to happen. She wouldn't let it! In innocent security of youth, I was convinced that my parents could fix everything!

The war pumped life into our local economy, and Dad was able to get increasingly more work as an electrician. With a bit more money coming in, we were able to move from our home on Cotton Mill Hill to a nicer place on Wilson Street. It was there that the war first affected my life.

Because he was married and now had a little girl, Ray could have received deferment from service in the war. We knew a lot of young men who had elected not to enlist in order to stay with their families. Nevertheless, my parents were not the least bit surprised when my oldest brother told them that he needed to fight for his country. He believed that the Younce family owed America a great deal, and it was up to him to pay back the country for the blessings it had given us. My thirteen-year-old mind couldn't comprehend the danger my brother would be facing, but I sure thought he looked good in a uniform.

As Ray headed off to Europe, I centered my attention on Brudge. I had always tagged after him. Now that he was in high school and the star of Lenoir's football team, I made sure that I followed him everywhere he went. The local newspaper had hung the handle of "The Educated Toe" on Brudge due to his success in the kicking game. As he won game after game with his accurate field goal kicks, Brudge's legend grew and so did my own bragging rights. I enjoyed the fame that was flowing off my brother's name and dripping down to mine. I was the "Toe's" little brother, and that made me special! In a very real sense, Brudge's exploits on the field meant more to me than even Ray's letters home. In my eyes Brudge was the Younce who seemed to be a real hero.

When I wasn't shadowing Brudge, I was with my dog. Jitterbug may have been just a duke's mixture, but I thought she had royal blood running through her veins. I wouldn't have traded her for Lassie or Rin Tin Tin. Whenever she had a litter of pups, I always acted like the proud father, showing each of the new pups to my friends. I would extol the new arrivals' blood lines and virtues and would brag that anyone who was fortunate enough to obtain one of these dogs was getting the very best the canine world had to offer. I must have been a pretty good salesman as I rarely had any trouble finding homes for the pups.

Jitterbug's first litter of 1944 was an extremely handsome group. Not only did a number of the local kids jump on the waiting list for one of then, but so did a man I didn't know from across town. While I had no problem "selling" folks on how good my dogs were, as any parent would, I had real problems actually letting my brood leave home. I would hold the chosen puppy for a long time before I turned it over to the new owner. Rather than watch the two of them leave, I would quickly turn and walk the other way.

One sunny, spring morning Mom reminded me that it was time to let go of another pup. I remember her singing as a neatly dressed man walked up to our yard. Sighing heavily, I waved, politely greeted him, and explained that the pups were under our front porch and it might take awhile to get them out. I was hoping he would change his mind, but he understood and informed me that he would wait until I could find one of them for him. Delaying as long as I could, I finally crawled under the house and scooted on my hands and knees back to where Jitterbug was hiding with her brood. I felt like a traitor as I pried one of the pups from her side. As both the pup and the mother dog mournfully stared at me, I felt a kind of sick feeling rumbling down in the pit of my belly. I sat there for at least a minute petting that tiny wiggling mass of fur and paws and hoping against all hope that the man would yell to me that he had changed his mind and would leave, but he never did. I had finally started to move back to the opening under the porch when I heard steps on the boards above my head. I stopped and waited as a loud knock on the door followed. Mom must have been in the kitchen. When she heard the knock, she stopped singing, then I heard her light steps as she walked to the front door.

"I have a telegram for you, Mrs. Younce," a voice softly announced.

For a few moments nothing happened. Then came the creaking of the screen door. I am sure that Mom's hands must have been trembling as she slowly and deliberately tore open the envelope. A few seconds later I heard her cry out. I knew what it meant. The war suddenly didn't seem so far away.

Tears streaming down my cheeks, I crawled out from under the porch and gave the puppy to the waiting man. I saw in the man's eyes an expression of absolute anguish. Helplessly he looked from my mother to me and back to her again. Shaking his head, he cradled the puppy in his arms and slowly walked away.

I don't remember Mom ever singing again. It seemed that she lost her song the moment she opened that telegram. For a while I did too. Suddenly all the games of my youth seemed unimportant. Ruthlessly, at the age of fourteen, I had been awakened to the cruelties of life.

Ray was buried in Italy. He didn't even get to come home to let us say good-bye. When the mailman delivered the flag that had been draped over his coffin, my mother cradled it as if it were her lost son. In her mind that red, white, and blue banner, a few faded photographs, and a name in a family Bible were all she had left of her oldest son. As the rest of us attempted to comfort her, to remind her of the good times, she seemed to sink deeper into her own world of grief.

Night after night I laid awake wondering what Ray's last days must have been like. He was so far from his family, facing death at every turn. He must have thought about his little girl a lot and wondered if she had taken her first step or spoken her first word. He also must have known how Mom worried. I wondered if he thought about all those milkshakes he had bought to make me into a Younce. My attempts to make any sense of Ray's death just confused and frustrated me. It wasn't fair. No matter how noble the cause, I believed his dying wasn't right. Yet maybe the thing that bothered me most was realizing for the first time in my life that Mom and Dad couldn't always fix everything. Even in the Younces' world bad things could happen.

It was probably no accident that less than a year after Ray was killed in battle I gave my heart to God during a Wednesday prayer meeting held in our home. My cousin Jay was preaching that service, but I had elected not to be a part of it. I had been sick all day, and my parents had allowed me to stay in bed, which was fine with me. Even though I had grown up in church and had been raised in a family who lived their faith, I had never made a public commitment to Christ. And I sure hadn't planned on making one that night.

Yet as my head throbbed and my body ached, I listened to each of Jay's words as they came through the wall. It was as if he had composed them just for me. Suddenly I could fathom what had never been real to me before. Perhaps I just hadn't been mature enough.

Being the baby of the family had not only spoiled me, it had also allowed me to slide by from time to time. Or maybe I began to understand the meaning of the gospel because of what Ray's death had done to my mother. Until this moment I don't think I had ever even considered what it meant for Jesus to die for me. Or maybe it was just the weight of a thousand sermons and twice as many gospel songs forming into a message that had dug deep enough to touch me. Or maybe it was just God's timing. For whatever reason, I suddenly realized that it was the Lord pounding on my soul's door. Jumping out of bed, I raced into the living room, bowed down, and asked Jesus into my heart. It was just that simple, and as I let the Lord in, I felt as free as I had felt when I once wandered the woods as a child. Mom and Dad might not have control over everything in life, but I now felt sure that God did!

A few years ago my brother Tommy called me to tell me that he had found the spring that had nourished our childhood. The first time I had a break in my schedule I returned to those woods with my own children and let my brother lead us to that old water hole. As I leaned down to drink the cool, refreshing water, something magical happened. For a few seconds, the years were washed away and I recalled simpler days. I could hear my mother's singing, my father's laugh, and even Jitterbug's bark. As I stared into the crystal clear water, I could see Ray's handsome face. Just as I had once looked at a radio set and had been able to picture those broadcasts so clearly in my mind, I now "saw" all the important lessons of my youth. I wish I could have told Mom that Ray's living and dying, my father's open arms, and her own singing had paved the way for my coming to Christ when I was fifteen. I realize that she now knows what I had never told her.

As I got up from the spring and walked back through the woods with my family, I realized something that proved a famous American author wrong: When you have the love of family and the faith of a child, it is never too late to go home again. God makes sure of that!

(chapter three)

HEAVEN ON EARTH

AFTER RAY DIED, things just weren't the same around the house. My brother's death left a huge hole that couldn't be filled by anyone or anything. I struggled for a year in my own juvenile fashion to come to grips with my loss while watching my mother do little more than go through the motions of life. Nothing that my father, Brudge, or I did could lift her dashed spirits. She would smile at us and pretend things were fine, yet while she still did a wonderful job of taking care of us and looking out for her neighbors and friends, I could tell that her heart was broken and she simply couldn't figure out how to put it back together again.

Our home had always been a place of music, but now when Mom cleaned, sewed, or cooked, she did it quietly. Even my happy-go-lucky ego had been brought down to earth by the melancholy spirit that hovered over our home. I came to realize after a while that it was her song that had brought me comfort, security, and sense of place. Without it I was lost. I wondered how long it was going to take for her to get it back.

During these days I spent many nights alone out on the porch looking at the stars. My school work, which had never been important to me, had become little more than an afterthought. I yearned to grow up and leave home. I wanted to find a new world where the sad ghosts of the past wouldn't haunt me. On most days I was like an old dog making his daily rounds, checking out the same things he had checked on the day before and the day before that. I was bored and gloomy.

At the end of the school term in 1945 I had nothing to look forward to but a long summer of doing nothing. I was too old to play in the woods, and jobs for unskilled kids were hard to find. I felt trapped. Though school had been out for barely a week, I already had worn out a pair of shoes just walking around town looking for something, anything at all, to occupy my time. Then a friend of mine asked me to ride with him up to Boone, North Carolina, where the Mayview Manor Blowing Rock Resort was hiring high school kids to work during the peak summer tourist season. I had heard stories about this place for as long as I could remember. The grand hotel was where Florida's rich folks came to spend their summers. Entranced by thoughts of watching the wealthy at play, I jumped at the chance to go with him.

When we arrived at the resort, I was mesmerized by the grandeur of the buildings and the fleet of Cadillacs, Lincolns, and Packards parked in the resort's paved parking lots. With impressive landscaped lawns and flower gardens, with lobbies and restaurants that looked to me like they belonged in European castles, I was completely awed by Mayview Manor. This world was so privileged and exclusive that I couldn't describe it with anything more than "Wow!" Here—even as the war for the world's freedom was still being fought on two fronts, even as thousands like my brother were dying each day—were hundreds of people who didn't have a care, lounging in comfortable lawn chairs, playing croquet, chatting in small groups, and racing off to the tennis courts. In the midst of all these society doings, I had arrived and caused not one of them to wonder what I was doing there. Though one glance would have told them.

I must have looked like the ultimate country bumpkin. Slack-jawed and decidedly underdressed by the standards of those who were amused by my gawking, I was definitely a fish out of water. Yet I was a bit too ignorant to know it. I even thought that this new "water" felt pretty good. I thought I would like to see if I could swim in this golden stream for a while. I could get used to this! So when the man who was interviewing my friend asked me if I would be interested in pulling kitchen duty for the summer, I smiled and nodded an enthusiastic yes.

We had one evening to drive home and then return to Mayview Manor. That scarcely gave us time to pack our clothes, much less say good-bye. It also didn't give my folks much time to talk me out of going.

Even though I assured my folks that I was going to be all right, that I had the chance to make good money, and I would be back home and headed back to school when the summer was over, I figured they would say no. Mom held out for a while, pleading in her soft voice for me to stay. Though she finally gave in, it must have broken her heart to have her baby leave the nest. She had tears in her red eyes as she watched me ride off the next morning. I barely had the courage to look back at her standing in the doorway. Yet as soon as we made it over the hill and out of sight of home, my mood changed dramatically.

I relished my luck at suddenly becoming a member of America's elite. I thought I was really in the chips. It was only after we had checked in with our supervisor, had been shown to our dormitory, which was well out of sight of the luxury accommodations at the manor, and I had been informed that I would be washing dishes ten hours a day, that I began to realize that my move uptown was not quite as big a move as I had thought.

For the next few weeks, I washed the remains of pheasant under glass and New York strip steak from china made in England. There, in front of a window overlooking Mayview's main entrance, I watched the limos arrive, the guests check in, and laughing, carefree souls spend hours leisurely doing as little as they could. As I studied their every move, I began to think I understood the ways of the idle rich. I also became convinced that I was getting to view heaven. For a while I even thought I was a part of it too. But after a few weeks of working seven days a week and only getting every other Sunday off, it dawned on me that I was seeing the kingdom from the outside looking in.

At night, in our dorms away from the main lodge, my life took on the vestiges of a summer camp. All the workers stayed in one large, two-story building, with the boys on the first floor and the girls on the second. We quickly became friends, and the veteran workers—the ones who had spent several seasons at the manor—tipped me off to the fact that friendly and considerate behavior could lead to some big tips as a waiter or busboy. Driven by the chance for some extra money and my desire to get closer to the upper class, I applied for a position as a waiter. By mid-summer I had earned a promotion but only to busboy.

Finally invited into the splendor of the dining room, I became the best busboy the Mayview had ever seen. Employing a technique

I had first learned as a dancing toddler, I quickly judged my audience, adjusted my personality, and played to the crowd. I was polite, respectful, and knew how to pass out solid compliments. I was so good at making the rich folks feel even more important that they began to drop large chunks of change my way. Within a week of beginning my tour of table duty I had made more money than I had in a month of washing dishes. Confident that this was just the beginning, I could see myself someday soon checking in to the manor and watching as some poor kid bused my table.

For the remainder of the summer, I dreamed about the good life and catered to the people who already had it. A world away from the sad memories of a brother who had died in the war, I celebrated victory in Europe and later victory in Japan with people who told good stories about what they had read in the newspapers but hardly knew the meaning of real sacrifice themselves. The fact that they didn't know how most of the world lived and suffered didn't bother me much, at least not as long as the big tips kept coming my way. And now that I was looking at this fine world up close from the dining room, I had almost convinced myself that I was a part of it. I had all but forgotten growing up barefooted on the poor side of town.

In late August I was taking a break just outside the kitchen when I noted a bit of commotion at the front entrance. There in the midst of the world's greatest luxury sedans sputtered a rusty old Model-A coupe, its engine struggling for breath and spitting gray smoke out the exhaust. *Someone must be lost*, I thought as I stared at the humorous scene. Grinning, I even pointed out the irony of such a pitiful heap parked next to all those rolling pieces of art. But as I climbed up on a fence to get a better look, my smile faded. Suddenly ashen white, I realized that the two hillbillies who were honking their horn to get my attention had come looking for me. Dressed in their Sunday best, hot and sweaty from their long, August drive, my parents had driven up for a visit. I was horrified.

Embarrassed by the man in the out-of-date suit and tie and the woman in the homemade print dress, I thought about running away rather than returning their greetings. *What are they doing here?* I wondered. *Don't they know that people are making fun of them?* Then, as they climbed out of the old car and came walking my way, I realized that I had been ready to make fun of them too. In three short months I had forgotten not only my roots, but my whole value system.

As Mom hugged my neck and Dad shook my hand, I shyly smiled and inquired as politely as I could, "What are you doing here?"

Mom explained, "We came to take you home, son. School will be starting next week."

Shaking my head, I stared at the magnificent buildings spread out around me and thought of the tips lining my pockets. I didn't want to give this up, especially not to go back to a life of going to school and making bits of pocket change by cutting trees and bailing hay.

"I'm not going back, Mom," I quietly muttered.

"What did you say, son?" My dad quickly cut in.

"I'm not going back to school or home." I almost whispered it. "The manor will keep me on here until they shut down at the end of October. I can make real good money, a lot better than I could ever make back home."

"But your schooling," Mom broke in.

"I will do just fine without it," I confidently stated, my voice now a bit louder. "Most folks who graduate from high school don't do as well as I am doing now. Maybe I can even catch on here for a long time. There are far worse places to live and work."

Mom and Dad pleaded with me for a good part of that afternoon before finally giving up and driving home. As the Model A moved off in the distance, a part of me yearned to be with them. I did miss my home, Mom's cooking, and going fishing with Dad and my brothers. I missed my friends too, yet I didn't miss anything enough to run after them—at least not that day. I wouldn't go home until Mayview Manor had closed its doors for the winter and all the fancy cars and rich people had followed the sun back to Florida.

When I finally returned to Lenoir, the holidays were all but upon us. In a lot of ways I hated those times. Thanksgiving and Christmas brought back memories of Ray lying in a grave in Italy. As much as Mom tried to make believe she wasn't feeling it too, I couldn't help but notice her staring at my brother's picture for a moment too long or glancing down the road as if looking for Ray to come walking home. My mother's pain was the main reason I spent a great deal of my spare time in other places. I couldn't stand watching her suffer and not being able to do anything about it.

I usually hung out with the Wilson brothers, a family from church who lived out in the country. They had been my best friends ever since we moved to Lenoir. Jovial pranksters, these brothers loved singing more than anything. I often would join them as they tried to work out harmonies on old gospel quartet songs. With my second tenor voice carrying the lead work, we convinced ourselves that we were pretty good.

In late 1945 the Wilsons invited me to go up the road to an old schoolhouse to hear a concert by the Harmoneers Quartet. I was game for most anything, so I agreed to ride along. We got there so early that I was able to get a front-row seat. Since I hadn't been to a live concert before, I didn't know what to expect. I certainly didn't know how I was going to react. I just knew that I was ready to feel good and have some fun—a little music, a few laughs, and a chance to be with friends. But when the quartet, made up of Fred Maples, Seals Hilton, Bobby Sticklin, Ermon Slater, and their piano player, Charles Keys, walked out onstage that night, something came over me. I felt chills, but there was no draft. My eyes pinched and strained, my throat went dry, and I couldn't swallow at all. For a second I even thought my heart had stopped. My hands began to sweat and my feet began to tap. And when the Harmoneers finally began to sing "I Am Glad My Savior Was Willing to Redeem My Soul," I thought I had died and gone to heaven. Suddenly, wanting to be one of the idle rich who summered at Mayview Manor was the last thing on my mind. I knew as I watched those men sing that I wasn't going to get to heaven in a Packard or a Lincoln; rather, I was going to make my trip riding a gospel song.

Overcome by the spirit of the evening, on the way home the Wilson boys and I decided to form a real gospel quartet of our own. No longer content to just sing around the house, we were determined to take our show on the road and into every church and school in the area.

My parents had never seen me this excited, at least not since I had become a teenager. I don't know if they believed me when I spoke of my dreams of singing on the radio and making records, but I do know that they were pleased that I was singing gospel music rather than running with the crowd that drank and caused trouble downtown each night. They probably also were thrilled that I was putting my dreams of wealth and big cars on the back burner.

I got a job washing rags for a furniture company during the day and began to spend each night working out harmonies with the Wilsons and their friends. By early 1946 we had dubbed ourselves the Spiritualaires and had landed a few gigs at singing conventions and small churches. I had never been so happy. At last I had a solid direction, a big dream to hang onto, and according to the people who heard me, a large talent.

For almost a year, I reveled in the group's growth and my own triumphs. I literally came alive onstage. It didn't make any difference if we were singing for twenty people or two hundred, when I was performing I felt as if I had jumped up to Glory. I sang in the bath, at work, and even in bed. I felt confident that I had discovered my personal niche and that this was what I would do for the rest of my life. As I watched my mother clap in time with our music, I even thought I had brought a bit of joy back to her life. I couldn't imagine life being any better.

Then one night as we performed in front of several hundred eager fans, my dreams and my confidence were suddenly shattered. While singing "Winging My Way Back Home," my voice cracked. I had to stop, clear my throat, and start again. Yet try as hard as I could, I couldn't find the notes. I stumbled through what became the longest evening of my life, hitting bad note after bad note. Everyone who heard us that night must have realized that I was the one messing up each song.

I knew that something serious was wrong. At first I blamed a cold and sore throat and convinced myself that a good night's sleep and a bit of honey and lemon juice would fix me up good as new. Yet it didn't, and at the next practice I came to realize the worst. My voice was changing; I could no longer hit the high lead notes. As the weeks passed, I found myself barely able to carry a tune. I was turning a solid vocal group into a laughingstock.

Ike Miller, the father of one of the boys in the group and the man who would become the Spiritualaires' guiding force, gently told me that I needed to take some time off. At sixteen years of age a week seems like forever, and Ike was telling me it was going to take a lot longer than that. I couldn't fathom what it would be like to wait months or even a year to find out if I would ever sing again. And I couldn't imagine my life without singing. The guys wanted me to stay on with the group even if I couldn't sing. They told me they needed my input on music and arrangements, but I knew better—they were just being nice.

Once again spiritually adrift, I worked my rag-washing job, spent a lot of time alone, and stayed as far away from gospel quartet music as I could. It hurt too much to listen to my friends practice or perform. I didn't even like to hear songs in church anymore. Now, just like my mother, I waltzed through life with no music.

In the brief span of a year, I had found and lost what I thought was heaven on earth, not once but twice. The first had been the world of material wealth, of lavish living and fancy cars. Now gone was a world of music that had brought great spiritual rewards. The second loss was far greater than the first. Not only did I not have the money to buy happiness, I didn't have the talent to earn it either. As I worked in the factory, I began to wonder if I would have been better off staying in school. If I had, I would have at least had some real career opportunities. Now it seemed that I was doomed to be the man on the bottom looking up.

Ike Miller checked on me from time to time. He always inquired about my voice, and I always replied with a shrug of my shoulders that it wasn't getting any better. Now almost seventeen, I terribly missed both being in front of the crowd singing with my friends and waiting on the guests at Mayview. As the days dragged by, I almost wished I had never gone to the Harmoneers concert and become so charged up about quartet music or taken a job that showed me all the fine things I didn't have.

As my life fell into its new routine, I grew to realize that I missed singing a great deal more than I missed my life at the manor. I also grew to know that it was very painful to have something on your heart and not be able to share it with the world. But at least I wasn't alone. I could look across the room at my mother and know that she understood how I felt. After all, her loss had been even greater than mine. And so we carried on our painfully muted duet, both searching for a way to give voice to our grief.

chapter four

"BOYS, WE ARE SOMEPLACE NOW!"

ONE DAY IKE MILLER stopped me on the street and asked me once again about my voice. I responded with a shrug of the shoulders, but he wouldn't accept that. He pestered me until I sang a few bars just to shut him up. As I warbled a few lines of an old hymn, his eyes grew as big as milk saucers, and his jaw dropped to his chest.

"Your voice is back!" he exclaimed with a gleam in his eye. "George, it's back!"

I shook my head, "There's a voice there, but it's not mine."

"Oh, yes it is, George," he laughed, "but you're not a tenor anymore; you're a bass singer."

I thought he was kidding me. Yet as I tried a few bass lines of another old hymn, I quickly realized that Ike was right. My voice had stabilized and dropped down so low that it was even lower than my father's. Immediately I remembered looking through the window of our church and watching Dad sing. *I can sing like him,* I thought. I have my wish! Who would have believed it? As a grinning Ike waved good-bye and walked off, I quickly turned and made a mad dash home. I couldn't wait to show off.

Out of breath after racing more than a mile, I tore through the house until I found my mother. Then, barely able to breathe, much less sing, I tried to belt out a few low notes. I probably sounded more like a mad bull than a bass singer, but she smiled anyway. Later, after I had caught my wind, I tried again, and this time she didn't have to pretend. No doubt about it—my voice had settled and matured.

That night I tried to sing every bass part out of every songbook we had in the house. Even though my parents smiled and told me how good I was, in retrospect I was probably pretty awful. I was doing a lousy job of reading the bass lines, and I wasn't hitting notes as much as I was sliding around them. Brudge was lucky that he was spending the evening out courting his girlfriend rather than listening to me reinvent bass singing. Still, as far as joyful noises go, my voice was happily butchering whatever I could find.

As the days passed and I grew more comfortable with my new sound, I began to get a feel for singing bass rather than lead. However, no one I knew of needed a bass singer, so I sometimes felt I was wasting my time. Just as I was growing tired of singing simply for my own pleasure, the bass singer for the Spiritualaires quit the group. The next time I heard from Ike Miller, he was asking me to come back to the quartet, but this time he wanted me to stand at the far end!

I was happier than I ever had been. It was as if heaven had opened again and swallowed me whole. I felt good all over, and I was singing everywhere I went. I didn't care who heard me or how many people thought the youngest Younce boy had gone crazy.

The group I now rejoined consisted of Stanley Wilson, tenor; Herb Miller, Ike's son, lead; Ike, baritone; myself, bass; and Willis Abernathy at the piano. Within a week of our first practice, I was dreaming big dreams again. I thought I had the tiger by the tail, and maybe I did. Who could have asked for a better life? With Ike footing the bill, almost every weekend the Spiritualaires sang at conventions or churches in Ashville, Statesville, Hickory, or a dozen other towns. With our blue pants and red shirts—made for us by Mrs. Miller—we looked sharp, and we must have sounded pretty good too, because people kept inviting us back for more.

I think Ike originally saw the gospel quartet as a way to keep his boy and his friends busy so we wouldn't have time to get into trouble. Yet as our sound improved, the harmonies growing tighter, it began to dawn on Ike that we had raw but real talent. As the months went by and our popularity grew, our mentor decided that he wanted to find a way to develop this raw talent into something more polished.

Ike came to us one day after a show and suggested that we make plans to go to the Stamps-Baxter Singing School in Dallas, Texas.

For me Dallas was on the other side of the world. I had never been out of the coastal hills, much less to the other side of the Mississippi. I couldn't imagine going that far just for a three-week school. But Ike assured me that it would be worth the time and the cost. Time I had, but the cost was something else.

When I got home that night, I told my parents about the school and how important Ike said it was. I didn't even think of asking for the tuition money. I realized that it was impossible; they simply couldn't afford it.

At our next practice, the other guys in the quartet were ready to go. They had their tuition money and bus fare and were looking forward to studying with the harmony masters of the time. I was a bit jealous. I guess I had always been poor, but up until this minute I hadn't realized how that limited me. Sure, I knew the rich folks at Mayview Manor were operating in a different world than I was, but I had always believed I had everything I needed. I also thought that I had everything my friends had. Now all that had changed. Just as 1 Corinthians 13 says, I had once seen things as a child, but now I could see the facts much more clearly: Being poor was a big handicap!

Mom and Dad must have had a lot of discussions about the school, but I didn't know about it. I just assumed that they had decided the cost was too much for people like us. But behind my back they were plotting. They knew all about the school because of the Stamps radio broadcasts. Deep inside they so badly wanted me to have a chance to go to the school that they were willing to take a huge step of faith to make it happen. I don't know what he used as collateral, and I certainly don't know how he talked the bankers into it, but Dad went down to the bank and borrowed enough money for my schooling, room and board, and bus ticket.

When I found out that Dad had managed to get the money, I didn't know what to say. I wanted to explode with joy, but I felt really bad. I couldn't imagine my parents going into debt for something as trivial as this. Nevertheless, they had made up their minds. Mom assured me that my attending the school was as big a dream come true for her as it was for me. She and Dad wanted me to learn more about this wonderful talent that brought such joy to my life.

Ike Miller felt sure that "his" boys were going to grow as never before through the experience of being on our own, traveling halfway across the country, seeing new things, and meeting new people. The added bonus of learning about music from the best would be the icing on the cake.

The next few weeks went by so slowly that I thought time had come to a stop. Finally, in June of 1947, I climbed onto a Greyhound bus with Stanley Wilson, Willis Abernathy, and Herb Miller, and we began a two-day trip to Texas. My mother was crying as I left. Though my smile exuded a sense of confidence, I was scared to death. There would be no coming home now.

For the first hours of the trip, my eyes remained glued to the passing countryside. I marveled at the huge trees in the Great Smoky Mountains, and I could hardly believe how long it was taking to cross Tennessee. It seemed like we stopped every five miles. Yet more than the sights I was seeing and the time it was taking, I couldn't believe how much my heart ached for home. By the time we reached Memphis, I was almost physically ill due to homesickness. If it was this bad on the bus, I wondered how I would survive once I made it to Texas.

It was twilight on Sunday night when we finally rolled into Dallas. The city's lights seemed to spread out forever. My mouth dropped open, and I shook my head at the size of the buildings and the hordes of people milling on the sidewalks. I had never seen so many movie theaters and so many different places to shop and eat. When we pulled into the downtown bus depot, I shyly stepped off the Greyhound into the hot summer air. Turning around, I craned my head, looked up, and caught a glimpse of a neon, flying red horse lighting up the city skyline from atop the Magnolia Oil Building. Laughing in childlike wonder, I motioned to my buddies and whispered, "Boys, we are someplace now!" I could tell by their slackened jaws and wide-eyed expressions that they agreed.

We made our way to Miller's Boarding House in Oak Cliff. Huddled together like frightened rabbits, we stood on the front porch waiting for someone to respond to our knock. In a few seconds, a big, jolly lady came to the door, studied us for a second, and then exclaimed in a loud voice, "You boys look like you are starved to death! I'll show you to your room, and then you come down to dinner."

The school had arranged for us to stay with Mrs. Miller, who quickly calmed our fears about Dallas, the school, and being away from our families. She also made us feel at home. Part mentor, part mother, and all cheerleader, she spent the first night building us up. Yet even after she had assured us that we were going to take the school by storm, I didn't sleep much. I didn't eat much breakfast the next morning either. I couldn't absorb Mrs. Miller's confidence. No matter what she said, I knew I was just a country hick way out of my element.

It was a bright Monday when we checked in at the church that housed the school. I had never seen a place so big! And it was air-conditioned too! The people in my little congregation wouldn't have known how to act in such a palace. I wasn't even sure I could describe it to them when I got home. Our entire membership could have met in the choir room and had enough seats left over for the Methodists too!

I quickly discovered that a large number of the more than one thousand people who were attending the school didn't have money for voice lessons. I wouldn't have had it either if Ike Miller hadn't signed me up and then paid for them out of his own pocket. Individual lessons cost a dollar a day, and at the time I thought it was an outrageous sum. Now I know that it was the best investment anybody ever made in me.

W. W. Combs was my voice teacher. Mr. Combs may have looked like Walter Brennen, but he was a gospel version of Beethoven. He knew his music. When he spoke I could see what he was talking about, for he painted a picture with his words. From the second I walked into his classroom, he began teaching me. He drilled it into my head to sing where I could be understood. To this day I still use the voice and diction exercises he started me on during that first lesson. Patient, kind, and yet demanding, he pushed me to give what even I didn't know I had. He also pushed me to read and understand what I was singing.

"George," he preached again and again, "it doesn't matter how low you can go or how loud you can sing; if the audience doesn't understand the song's message, you have wasted your time and their time. In gospel music it is the words that matter. Your diction must be perfect!" Every day Mr. Combs dwelled on how to shape each note and phrase. He wanted to make sure I understood how important diction and delivering the message really was.

Vidette Polk was my music teacher and was even smarter than Mr. Combs. He could write down a song, read it, and sing it before I could even mumble through the first verse. He wasn't afraid to show me that he had forgotten more than I would ever know. Strict and precise, he was somebody with whom you didn't clown around. After my first attempt at humor fell flat, I surmised that this handsome, medium-sized man, always dressed in a freshly pressed suit, was too committed to teaching me music to have time to laugh or even smile. He was a musical drill sergeant. In three short weeks I went from knowing how to turn to a song in a book by finding the number at the top of the page to learning to read, write, and understand everything that was printed on each page of a hymnal. I left his class on the second day having learned more about music than I had learned in my first seventeen years of life. By the end of the three weeks, I felt as though I could teach music to college students!

Besides Mr. Combs and Mr. Polk, I met and worked with so many gospel music legends that I scarcely can remember them all. Leroy Abernathy, who had written such classics as "Wonderful Time Up There," worked with our quartet, as did Elmo Fagg, one of the best-known quartet singers of the era. I couldn't believe how nice these people were to me and all of the other green hicks who had come out of the backwoods in hopes of improving their singing. As much as I learned about music, these great people taught me even more about the joys of helping others.

With group classes, singing lessons, voice lessons, and a host of other special study courses, I didn't have time to get homesick. I was running from the moment I got up until the moment I went to bed. And as busy as I was through the week, life was even more frantic on Saturday and Sunday!

On the weekends we would load into buses and travel to other towns to participate in singing conventions. These dawn-to-dusk gatherings drew thousands and made our previous experiences back home look pretty anemic. As I joined in on some of the greatest gospel songs of all time sung by hundreds of trained voices singing as one, I was completely blown away. Chills running up my spine, I couldn't imagine the choirs of Glory ever sounding this sweet, full, and powerful. I never wanted these sessions to end. When they did,

I was still so caught up in the spirit of it all that I had trouble going to sleep. Long after my roommates were dreaming dreams of home, I was still quietly humming bass lines.

When the school term ended, we all gathered at the Sportatorium—a huge arena usually reserved for boxing and wrestling—to show off what we had learned. The singing would go on all night and would even be broadcast on KRLD radio, one of the nation's most powerful stations. Yet more exciting than graduating from the Stamps-Baxter school was the fact that the Spiritualaires were one of the featured acts on the bill. In addition to the ten thousand people in the live audience, we were actually going to sing for the nation. Our families and friends back home would get to hear us too.

I called Mom and Dad and informed them that we would be on the air in the wee hours of the morning. Mom was so excited that she tuned in KRLD three hours early, sat in front of our small radio, and refused to move. She also prayed for everything from the weather—she didn't want any lightning storms messing up the signal—to the old set itself. For hours she watched the clock and waited. For the first time in my parents' marriage, my dad would have to help himself if he wanted something from the kitchen. Mom was not going to do anything but stare at the radio and keep everyone quiet.

But while Mom was excited, I was scared to death. As our time to perform drew near, I felt sicker and sicker. I just knew I was going to throw up. Looking around, I noted that the other guys appeared to be in just as bad shape as I was. We all wanted to back out but couldn't!

When the master of ceremonies finally announced our name and the four of us mounted the stage, I went completely blank. In one instant I forgot everything I had learned in three weeks of schooling. As I looked out on the thousands of faces studying us, I was vaguely aware of Willis's piano introduction. Sweat shooting from every pore in my body, I began to sing when my buddies did, but I had no idea what I was singing. As the chills ran up my spine, I tried to hit note after note, yet I didn't know if I was succeeding. I couldn't seem to hear the other guys or even hear myself. I must have sounded like Daffy Duck.

Surrounded by the best in the business, we all felt great pressure. We sounded pretty good when we sang in the small Carolina churches that were home to us, but we couldn't begin to believe we came anywhere close to the singers who were on the bill with us that night. To sing at that moment was torture, the longest three minutes of my life!

I guess there was applause when we finished our number, though I don't remember it. I don't remember finding my seat either. A couple of the other guys later told me that they didn't even remember being onstage. To this day I can't recall the song we sang, but we must have made it through it. At least my mother told me she thought we were great! When Mom had heard us on the radio, she had been so proud she cried. I wondered if Mr. Polk and Mr. Combs had shed a few tears too—for other reasons.

Even though we all felt we had blown our moment in the spotlight, we came home ready to sing up a storm. We wanted to take the group to new heights. And because of what we had learned, our sound was not only much better, but so was our message. No longer were we a sloppy, sliding group of kids, we were much more polished and precise. We could also read music almost as well as we could read lyrics. We really had grown a lot.

One of those who caught our act and was impressed with our new sound was the manager of the local radio show. In the fall of 1947, WHKY in Hickory gave us fifteen minutes of radio time every Sunday morning. Beginning each broadcast with our theme song, "Grand and Glorious Feeling," we hit the airwaves with a string of gospel classics, such as "Gonna Ride That Glory Train," "Go Right Out," "A Rainbow of Love," and "Roll On Jordan." Our show soon became the focal point of many people's Sunday mornings. As we sang in singing conventions and outdoor meetings throughout the area, fans of all ages came up and told us how much our little show meant to them. People were predicting that we were soon going to be regional stars with our own record contract!

At seventeen I figured I was now a pretty important person. I had tasted a bit of local fame and, along with my buddies, I had my own radio show. At concerts pretty, young girls waited to meet me. Older folks told me that I was blessing their walk with the Lord. Yet as good as things were in public, at home it was even better.

I couldn't help but note the effect my music was having on my mother. Though she still wasn't singing, she seemed to get a great deal of joy from just listening to me. I thought, as did my father, that the Spiritualaires' music was helping to heal her heart.

Almost a year after I attended the Stamps-Baxter school, I was still riding this grand wave of personal satisfaction and success. I had been promoted to a better job in the furniture factory, the radio show and concert dates were going stronger than ever, and I was looking at a future that held great promise. I think I actually believed that I was going to be a star. Yet as so often happens when a person is riding so high that he figures he is in complete control of his life, the bottom falls out. That is exactly what happened to me in 1948.

Often when we practiced or returned home from a show late, I wouldn't go home to sleep. I would always tell Mom and Dad ahead of time so that they wouldn't worry. On this particular evening, I stayed all night with the Wilson boys. For all practical purposes, this night seemed no different than any other. The guys and I had worked on a few songs, listened to a new recording by our favorite group, the Blue Ridge Quartet, and had drifted off to sleep sometime after midnight. Things changed dramatically when just before dawn Mr. Wilson came into the boys' room and softly shook me awake.

"George," he whispered as I rubbed the sleep out of my eyes. "Son, I hate to tell you this," he continued, his voice struggling to gain some kind of strength, "but your mother died last night. Your dad found her dead in their bed this morning. You need to go home, son."

I couldn't believe it. Just yesterday she had seemed fine; it had to be a mistake. Yet as I looked into Mr. Wilson's pained and drawn face, I realized there had been no mistake: She was dead.

I got up and silently dressed. Mr. and Mrs. Wilson watched me with sad eyes as I tiptoed out their door. It was almost as if I were sleepwalking. At first I felt nothing. Then, as I walked down the hill to my home, a sense of dread filled my soul and a thousand memories flooded my mind. I couldn't imagine life without Mom. I felt like a little boy again. I felt hopeless, lost. I wanted to run away. Yet rather than run, I finally worked up the courage to walk up on the front porch and greet my father.

My father, sister, and brothers seemed to share my wandering emotions. None of them knew what to do or say. We talked about how Mom would want her funeral, and we remembered the way she was, but none of us showed our true feelings. We were just too numb. Because her death had come so quickly, we simply hadn't had time to prepare or to say good-bye.

Mom's funeral a couple of days later was just like all the others I had seen. Because I was still numb, I really don't remember much about it. While the hymns were sung and messages delivered, I couldn't stop thinking of all the times Mom had dragged me out of church because I wouldn't sit still. At that horrible moment, I wished she had been there to drag me out just one more time.

A lot of people flooded our house with food and sympathy after the service. One of those who tried to assure me that everything was going to be all right was my dad's brother. Not long after he talked to me about faith and hope, he walked out into the front yard, suddenly grabbed at his chest, and dropped dead. His death was another burden, a sure sign that it was going to take a long time for any of us to be happy again.

For a while, it was just Dad and me at the house. Brudge had recently gotten married, and sensing that Dad and I weren't doing too well, he moved his new bride back home to help take care of us a few weeks after the funeral. I was glad for Dad's sake that Brudge and Mozell had decided to pitch their tent with us.

For the next year of my life, I worked my day job, sang with the Spiritualaires, and looked for a way to escape going home. I stayed with friends when I could. And when I did have to go home for a night, I would put it off for as long as I could. Many evenings I would find a deserted street, sit against an old tree on the damp evening grass, and count the stars. I guess I was feeling sorry for myself, but there was more to my extended mourning than selfish emotion.

By not going home, I was trying to escape the feelings of not having thanked my mother for all that she had done for me. I felt that I had not done enough to help her get over the loss of Ray. I also felt guilty for not being home the night she died. Perhaps what made me feel worst was knowing that now that she was gone I was helpless to fulfill any of my dreams of making her proud of me. If she wasn't going to be there to see me sing in front of thousands of people, what was the real use in doing it?

Dad picked up his life better than I did. He quickly worked his way up to being the city's electrical inspector. With Brudge and Mozell around him, he even started to laugh again. He somehow sensed that in death Mom had found the peace she had lacked the last few years of her life. While I believed that in my heart, my mind wouldn't let my own personal doubts subside. It seemed that my faith had been shaken clear down to its foundation.

I didn't know that the answers to all of my doubts and fears were all around me. They were in the Bible that sat beside my bed and in the words of the songs I sang on the radio with the quartet. At that time I thought the only way I was going to find the answers I needed was to go somewhere else, do something else, maybe even be someone else. I vowed that when I got my chance, I would do all of those things. For now I simply strolled silently through my life.

So quickly after I had found it again, it seemed that I had lost my song. I wondered if I would ever get it back.

chapter five

SPREADING MY WINGS

I n 1950 I was pretty much treading water. I had lost a lot of my enthusiasm for life and just couldn't seem to get it back. I was looking for something but didn't know what it was, and I certainly didn't think I was going to find it anywhere close to home. I was tired of everything I was doing, even tired of being in church and singing in a quartet. I had lost the ability to embrace anything with my whole heart.

A close friend from West Virginia, Bill Devlin, had been drafted. For the few weeks before Bill was to be shipped out, he and I had spent a lot of time together talking about life. I envied the fact that he was getting away from home. He was about to live an adventure while I was going to do the same things over and over again every day. As I told him how fortunate he was, I had no way of knowing that I was the lucky one: Meeting Bill and becoming his friend was not only going to radically change my life in the present, but in the future as well.

When it came time for Bill to be inducted officially into the service, he asked me to ride with him to Charlotte. Having nothing better to do, I went along. As I watched Bill check in at headquarters, I began to talk to a man who was in charge of area recruiting. He was smooth. As we sat there, he spun tales of the excitement and adventure of being in the army. He talked about all the great things I could learn and all the places I could see. The more he explained about this wonderful life, the more interested I became.

I began to wonder why Bill had waited to be drafted. The life this guy was describing sounded great! My friend was going to get a great education and a lifetime of practical experience, as well as make countless new friends and see the world in the process. And this guy swore that being in Korea was safer than driving a car in a big city. Everything Bill needed was going to be taken care of for him. To hear this recruiter tell it, Bill was not going to have to do anything for himself. At least that is the way it sounded to this gullible country boy.

Within thirty minutes of arriving in Charlotte, I had picked up a pen, signed my name on enlistment papers, and was on my way with Bill. Right before I left, I called home and proudly told my dad that I was in the army. He was more than a little shocked, yet as I explained what I had done, he realized it was too late to talk me out of it. I was stuck. He wished me well and told me to do my best. I assured him that I would.

In retrospect I am glad that my mother wasn't around to go through the trauma of having another son in the military, but the thought that I might end up like Ray never entered my mind. In fact, I'm not sure much of anything entered my mind during that time. If it had, I would have waved good-bye to Bill and headed back home.

It didn't take long for me to begin to rethink my spur-of-the-moment decision. Within days of my joining the army, I had been sent to Fort Campbell, Kentucky, where I was given my first army vocational training course. All day long, day after day, I pulled grass and weeds with my hands. Rather than seeing the world, all I had managed to see were the backsides of dozens of other young guys who were learning this trade along with me. Never in my life had I worked so hard doing something so totally unconstructive. Each night as my back ached and my hands throbbed, I lay awake on my bunk wishing I were back home with my family.

After more than a week of lawn care, my group was assembled and addressed. A smooth-talking sergeant (I would later believe he was related to the recruiter) explained that the army needed volunteers to jump out of airplanes. When he went on to point out that they were going to be nice enough to furnish all of the jumpers with parachutes, my interest perked up. By the end of his spiel I had signed some more papers and found myself a member of the 82d Airborne Division. Once again I had no idea what I was doing or what I was in for.

I had never even stepped into a plane before I went to para-troopers school. Since the army was serious about the training of paratroopers, I was to go up in a plane fifteen times before I ever landed in one. As I looked down for the first time at the earth thousands of feet below me and watched our first man jump, I thought, *Man I have got to be crazy.* Suddenly, pulling weeds looked good. But there was no backing out. When it was my turn, I took a deep breath and ran out the door. Then as I waited for my chute to open and take hold, I rededicated my life to Christ. No sermon had ever had the spiritual power that jumping out of an airplane had. I know the saying that there are no atheists in foxholes, but it is also really hard not to be a believer when you are throwing yourself out of an airplane.

With the Korean conflict building, most of us were convinced that our 504-E Company would end up in the thick of battle. We looked for the orders every day, but they never came. Instead, as part of Operation Snowshoe, we were shipped to northern Canada. There my company made a jump in full snow equipment. Over the next week we camped out in the snow, ice, and wind. I found out only after we had hit the ground that the temperature wasn't going to rise above thirty degrees below zero. During that week, the army monitored us to find out how well prepared we were for fighting the enemy in a place like Siberia. If they had asked me, and they didn't, I would have been glad to tell them that it would be a good idea to fight the next war someplace warm. If some country wanted to own a bunch of snowdrifts and polar bears, let them!

Evidently satisfied that we could survive in the cold, the army then decided to drop us in the desert. That alone didn't bother me. I figured I could survive the heat, lizards, and snakes much better than the cold. What was really scary about this mission was that we were being dropped into an area that had recently been part of an atomic bomb test. So now we were being monitored to see what we could manage if we fought a ground war in an area ripe with radiation. Besides the men, the army also dropped in goats. I guess they wanted to see what would happen to them if they ate some of the "hot" material. To this day I don't know what became of the goats, but I clearly remember that I spent my week in the desert picking up and piling rocks, a duty even worse than pulling weeds.

I now know how fortunate I was not to have acquired radiation poisoning or cancer. A lot of guys weren't as fortunate. I believe the

Lord kept an eye on me during this time. Rather than looking toward heaven and thanking God for protecting me, however, my own eyes were focused on earthly things.

When I wasn't jumping, I was assigned special duty—working in an NCO club at Fort Bragg as a bartender and short-order cook. Seeing the same kind of opportunities behind the bar that I had once seen on the cotton mill walk, I entertained the men to earn tips. Whenever they requested a favorite song, I gladly obliged. I performed gospel, country, pop, and even some comedy numbers. My bass voice became so well known that I was asked to join a country band that performed regularly at the club.

For the next couple of years, I sang with Homer Briarhopper and His Briarhoppers. This is what kept me at Fort Bragg; I became such a favorite with the officers that I was never transferred. I never got close to Korea or any other foreign base, but rather than being a real favor, this act of kindness nearly became my spiritual and physical undoing.

The church and gospel music had been the focal points of my life for as long as I could remember, but in the service I pushed what had once been the most important areas of my life to the back burner. I became just another one of the guys. As I worked in the bar, I was surrounded by alcohol. It didn't take long for me to trade in my glass of Coca-Cola for a shot of whiskey or a cold mug of beer. When soldiers offered to buy me a drink so that I would listen to their problems, I convinced myself that it wouldn't be right to turn them down. And when I was offered a drink for singing a song, I took it.

I didn't realize what was happening at the time, that over the months I had been drinking far too much. Yet within a year of enlisting, I was all but drowning in booze. During the day I didn't show it; no one around me would have guessed I had become addicted. But at night it was a different story; my addiction had grown to the point where I had to have a drink just to sleep. I started to take a bottle of whiskey to my bunk every night. At first I would take a quick belt and sleep through until morning. Over time that one belt became two and then three. Eventually I would wake up in the middle of the night and have to take a drink just to stop the shakes. As the shakes grew worse and the darkness more terrifying, I was forced to make sure I took the cap off the bottle before I went to sleep. Otherwise I might have had to break the bottle just to get it open when my need woke me up.

I couldn't believe how quickly I had fallen victim to influences around me. I had bought the paratrooper myth that the only way to be a real man was to fight, cuss, and drink. I had so much wanted to fit in with this crowd that I became one of them, easily turning my back on everything I knew was right. The more I drank, the more I found I was able to justify anything I did.

For the remainder of my days in the service, I swam in booze. It was as much my life as gospel music once had been. Yet in this case, I hated myself for it. I left home to find myself, and I didn't like the guy I had discovered. Prior to joining the service, I wouldn't even have run around with someone like me.

I don't know what would have happened to me if I had stayed in the service. All of the officers tried to get me to reenlist. In a lot of ways I had an easy life, so it was tempting. Yet somewhere in my heart, buried under a lot of bad experiences, a voice was crying out to me to come home. And it was that little voice, planted through the Christian influences of a family that loved me, that allowed me to walk away from both the army and booze.

My first Sunday back home I strolled into the church I had known my whole life and looked at the people who always had been part of the congregation. As the familiar, old songs were played and the preacher preached, I took a good look at what I had become. I didn't like me one bit. That little voice in my heart that had brought me home was now crying out louder. Though no one around me knew it, a personal war was being fought inside my heart at that very moment. This silent but very violent war would shape my entire life from that moment on. If I had turned a deaf ear to that small voice, if I had walked out of church that day without acknowledging my problem and my own inability to solve it, I don't know what would have happened to me. I probably would have sought out the nearest still or bar and taken a large swig of liquid security. But rather than walk out after the invitation, I walked forward during it.

Falling on my knees at the front of the church, I gave my life to God. With emotions flooding my soul, I turned my burdens over to him. In the process of just a few seconds, all of my problems seemed to fall into perspective. Immediately I lost the urge to drink. At that moment, I also finally accepted my mother's death for the first time.

Though I had jumped out of scores of planes and pushed my way through countless manly exercises during my days in the service, until I fell to my knees, I had been a boy. I had thought as a child, walked as a child, and had the spiritual maturity of a child. I had always looked for immediate gratification and satisfaction. I had dreamed big dreams but had never really put great effort or faith into achieving them.

Now as I walked out of church, I saw the world differently. I knew I was going to have to earnestly pray and then work hard to make something meaningful of myself. I was also going to have to look for the opportunities the Lord was going to give me. I was finally ready to find the real George Younce and see what kind of guy he could be.

Many people find it hard to believe that once I gave my heart back to the Lord I never had the desire to take another drink. I could sleep through the night, watch others drink, and even walk into a place that served alcohol and never feel a single craving. I believe to this day that the power of the Lord is so strong that any problem— no matter how great—can be turned over to him and be made manageable. I also know that if I hadn't come home, reconnected with the people who accepted me as being just plain old George, and reinstituted the practices and beliefs of my childhood, I would have been lost in the bottle forever. Thus, I not only discovered the healing power of God when I walked the aisle and rededicated my life to him, but I also fully understood the need for all of us to surround ourselves with positive Christian influences all the time. Without those influences, it becomes very easy for any of us to stray from what we know is right. I had experienced this firsthand.

Shortly after I returned home, I went back to work in the furniture factory. The wages were low, but the work was steady and I liked the people with whom I worked each day. I probably would have stayed with that job for years if an old friend from my years at the NCO club hadn't called.

Sergeant Ramsey was one of the soldiers who had taken a shine to me at Fort Bragg. He had been one of the men who pulled strings to keep me from being transferred. Now that he was out of the service, he and a couple of his friends had gotten wind of a job in Alaska that was paying incredible wages. They had signed up for construction work and had come by to tell me that I needed to go with them. Just as I had been completely taken in by the recruiting officer's spiel a few years earlier, I was captivated by Ramsey's confident vision of life in Alaska. As I packed my bags, I saw this new job as picking up gold from the sidewalks.

We drove to Alaska in the sergeant's brand new DeSoto. The first part of the trip was fine, but once we got to Canada, the bottom literally dropped out. Many of the roads we were forced to take were little more than animal trails, and there were times when we were lucky to make ten miles an hour. When we finally made it to Alaska, it was even worse. We busted a gas tank, tried to paste it together with GI soap, and when that didn't work, we wasted a couple of days finding someone to weld it. What scared me to death about the old fellow who undertook that job was that he didn't even bother draining the tank before he went to work. I was more nervous watching him take a torch to the DeSoto than I had been when I was jumping out of a plane over an A-bomb sight. The pains and trials of this trip should have shown me that the Lord didn't want me in the north country. Yet for some reason, after the gas tank was fixed, I kept going.

When we finally arrived in the mountains of Alaska, I discovered that the Palmer Construction Company really expected me to work. In fact, they put me in a shaft two and a half miles underground and gave me a shovel. I was assigned to help dig a two-mile tunnel through a mountain to a lake in order to bring water to a hydroelectric plant on my side of the mountain. On top of that, when I looked at the contract I had signed, I realized that as soon as we were finished in Alaska I had guaranteed that I would travel to South America to work on a project down there. I was trapped for at least the next two years of my life. As I worked in the pitch blackness of the pit, I wondered aloud, *George what have you done to yourself now?*

As much as I didn't care for jumping out of a plane two and a half miles in the sky, I liked digging in dirt two and a half miles down in the earth even less. For one month I did my best imitation of a human mole and then called it quits. I settled up with the company for the price of a ticket home. They got a lot of hard work out of me for that small amount of cash, but I wouldn't have it any other way. When the bus pulled into my hometown, I never felt so relieved.

Immediately and gladly, I went back to work in the factory. This time I had a fond feeling for all the dirt, sand, and varnish. After being under the ground, this line of employment looked really good to me. My job title was a sander, but in truth I was an extra man. The foreman was our neighbor, and he liked me, so every day I spent a great deal of time waiting while he and his men sanded a piece of wood. When they finished, I took it to the truck. In order to make time pass more quickly, I sang for them whatever song they wanted to hear. I soon discovered that I was more of an entertainer than a line worker. This seemed perfectly fair to me; after toiling as hard as I had in Alaska, I thought I deserved a break.

The real focal point of my life during these days was not my work. Every afternoon when the final whistle blew, I displayed far more energy than I ever did on my job by high-tailing it out of the plant as fast as I could. Cutting across alleys and backyards, I raced back to Dad's house at break-neck speed. Flying through the living room, I threw the old radio's switch up as high as it would go just so I could catch the Blue Ridge Quartet on WSPA. Lying on the floor, my breath coming in short, shallow bursts, I listened to the sounds of the gospel harmony that had once been such an important part of my own life. How I missed it. Singing for a few guys at the factory just wasn't the same as cutting loose with three other guys on a gospel standard. Deep down I knew I had an even greater addiction to quartet music than I ever had to booze. Sadly, I just couldn't find a way back into the gospel music scene as easily as I could have found a bottle. It seemed that no one was looking for a good bass singer. Yet even though I couldn't do what I really wanted, I was smart enough to know that I was much more fortunate than a lot of guys my age.

In fact, Bill Devlin, the friend who had been instrumental in getting me into the service, had been in a battle for his life in Korea while I was fighting a battle with the bottle and entertaining officers at Fort Bragg. He lost his battle. I always felt guilty that this fine guy had died and I hadn't even been a part of the fight that had taken his life. He had paid such a high price, and it seemed that I had paid nothing.

Not long after I returned from Alaska, I found out where Bill's parents lived in West Virginia, and in 1953 I also ran into one of his friends who was on his way to see the Devlins. I hitched a ride on that Saturday just so I could tell Mr. and Mrs. Devlin how much their son had meant to me and how fine a young man he was. When I arrived at the house, I met more than the Devlins. Arthur Herald, Jack Clark, and Mason Lilly were using the Devlins' living room to rehearse a few gospel numbers. They were members of a group that performed in churches and at singing conventions in the area. As they worked their way through the numbers, I realized they were pretty good.

They must have noticed I was humming along with them, because one of them asked if I had ever sung gospel music. I modestly replied that I had once been a part of a quartet in my own hometown.

"Well," Mason said, "let's see what the boy's got."

I joined in on the next few numbers. At that time I had no idea that the trio had recently been a quartet but had lost their bass singer. Neither did I realize they were about to make me an offer I couldn't refuse.

"George," Arthur said after he and the guys had held a powwow, "we like your style. Your voice blends well with ours. Why don't you come sing with us? We can't pay you anything, but we can give you room and board and enough cash to see a movie or buy a Coke once in a while. You can live with me and my wife. And we guarantee that you will get the chance to sing a lot of good gospel music."

I was making fair money at the furniture factory without working very hard to earn my check. And life was pretty easy at home too. I wouldn't be lying if I said that few house cats had it any better. Yet when these boys offered me the opportunity to sing gospel music for nothing, I accepted on the spot. Was this a smart, well-conceived move? Of course not! But it was the best thing that ever could have happened to me. Finally, I was leaving home for all the right reasons and looking for the answers in all the right places.

As I returned to Lenoir and packed my bags to move to Glenfork, West Virginia, I realized that Bill Devlin was still playing a role in my life. He had been instrumental in my getting in the army. In the service I had fought my own battle, had lost a bit of myself and my soul, but had come out wiser and more mature. The experiences

I had suffered through in the army had led to my becoming a stronger Christian once I got out. Now my faith was stronger and my connection with Bill was leading me into another kind of service, this time for the Lord. I knew I was taking a huge leap of faith by joining the Watchmen, but I didn't have a clue as to what it was going to mean to my life. I did know that it was pretty stupid to leave a job that paid to take one that didn't. But if I had done the smart thing and played it safe, I never would have met my wife or Glen Payne and never would have become a member of the Cathedral Quartet.

To this day I owe Bill Devlin a lot. Because of him, I met the men who gave me a chance to pursue my dream and find myself. It had to be the Lord's hand that led me to Charlotte and then to Glenfork. It had to be the Lord who made sure Bill found his way into my life when I needed him most.

{ *chapter six* }

THE WATCHMEN

THE WATCHMEN OPENED UP new doors for me. I was singing a wider variety of songs and performing more frequently as part of a group that seemed to me to be headed for the "big time." At that moment the "big time" simply meant performing in a church that was large enough and rich enough to have their own in-house baptistery, unlike small churches that ushered their new converts out to the nearest river for baptism.

Arthur Herald's wife had sewn us red shirts to wear with blue pants, so we looked as sharp as we sounded. Enthusiastic and energetic, we were also musically pretty solid from top to bottom. We not only managed good harmonies, but our personalities blended well too. When spending as much time as I was with these men, the latter was almost as important as the former. Doing something I enjoyed with people I liked made me happier than I had been in years.

Since we performed at night and on weekends, I filled my daytime hours listening to the radio, doing odd jobs, and helping take care of the Heralds' toddler, Jimmy. Doris needed someone to help watch Junior so she could do her household work, so I volunteered, thinking it was an easy way to both give her a break and relieve my daytime boredom. *Besides*, I thought, *how hard can keeping up with a toddler be?*

For the next few weeks, my life resembled a Hollywood comedy. I chased Jimmy everywhere. If I turned my back for a second, he was in the next room. About the time I relaxed enough to pick up a newspaper or magazine, I would hear a crashing noise coming from another part of the house. Even though I loved the little guy, I soon found out that he was running me ragged. My entire army division couldn't have kept up with Jimmy's maneuvers. The more the child exhausted me, the more I began to wonder how my mom had managed to keep up with me in my youth, for I had been more energetic and troublesome than Jimmy.

After a few weeks of picking up after this diminutive dynamo, anything, including other household chores, began to look good to me. With that in mind, I negotiated a change in my daytime routine. I "explained" to Doris that it would be good for her to have more quality time with Jimmy, and I could give her that time by shouldering some of the housework and laundry. As she handed me a mop and took Jimmy into her arms, I couldn't help noticing that Doris seemed a bit too pleased to make the trade.

If taking care of a toddler was tough, then helping with the housework pointed out how difficult it was to be a housewife. Doris had no dishwasher, vacuum cleaner, or miracle cleaning solutions. Pots and floors had to be scrubbed, rugs had to be beaten, and clothes had to be washed the old-fashioned way. That meant building a fire under a huge, black kettle filled with water and soap and pushing the clothing around with a long wooden rod, a hot, back-breaking exercise. Then came hanging the heavy, wet items on the line, taking them down, and pressing them with an iron heated over a flame. I even learned how to make clothes look brand new by dying them. The more I worked, the more I fell behind. How I longed for the easy life at the furniture factory.

I decided that Doris must really love Arthur to sign up for a lifetime of such difficult work. At that time, I just couldn't fathom how any woman would ever love me enough to literally kill herself just keeping a home and family in shape. Until then, I hadn't met anyone who would volunteer for that duty either. At the rate I was going, I didn't figure I ever would.

When I wasn't helping around the house, I was hanging out with Arthur at his used-car lot. As an avid talker and good storyteller who liked to please people, I seemed naturally suited for sales. There was only one problem: I had a huge personality flaw that would have kept me from making money in the business. Though I was pretty good at pointing out a vehicle's good features, I was even better at pointing out the flaws. Hence, about the time I had somebody sold on a car, I would talk him or her out of buying it. So much for my career in business!

In spite of my tour of duty as a maid and nanny, I simply couldn't imagine life getting any better. The other guys in the quartet were great, and I could feel myself maturing as a bass singer. I could also sense that the audience was responding to my talents as well. Each appearance seemed stronger than the night before. I couldn't wait to go onstage.

One night in August 1954 I was feeling really good about my voice and my work. I just knew that the people who would be listening that evening would be mightily impressed! To use modern terminology, I was in the "zone." We were singing in a church before an audience of about seventy-five people. Though their numbers were small, the enthusiasm was incredible. Throughout the little sanctuary, faces were lit up and smiles covered the room. The audience amened and applauded after every song, even joining in on familiar numbers. As our performance continued, I couldn't help but get pumped up.

Whenever I sing, I try to make eye contact with as many people as I can. I want to look into their faces and read their reactions. When I see that people are being blessed by what we are doing, I draw from that; it gives me energy. By the middle of our first set, I had worked my way through almost all the pews. Then, right before we launched into an old Brumley classic, I noted a few young people standing at the back of the church. Turning my attention to them, I smiled as I sang and looked one by one into their faces. I was about halfway through the group when I saw *her*.

I didn't know who she was, I only knew that she was the most beautiful woman I had ever seen. She carried herself with a grace and dignity that I had never noticed in a young person. Her hair looked so soft and she stood so straight. Her eyes sparkled and her face glowed. I could tell that she had confidence and brains, and she was the most perfect vision I had ever beheld. If the song we were singing hadn't been so familiar, I am sure that I would have stumbled all the way through it. Just looking at her made my knees weak.

For the rest of the night, I sang to no one else. I stared directly at her and sang directly to her, yet in all the time I studied her, I couldn't read how she was responding to me or to our songs. I was getting no feedback. It was as if this beautiful girl was a picture without life. At least she didn't seem to have any life for me.

After the service had concluded and almost before the last note faded, I cut through the crowd and down the aisle toward the door where I had seen the girl step outside. Standing on the church steps, I searched through the night shadows in an effort to pick her out of the crowd milling around the cars in the parking lot. I finally spotted her next to an old sedan, where she stood visiting with some of the other kids who had stood against the back wall during our songs. Doing my best to appear cool and calm, I strolled over to the group.

"Hi," I said using the lowest voice I could manage. I was sure this would impress her. It had always worked before.

Of the four or five kids in the group, all but one of them responded enthusiastically to my greeting. The one who didn't had buckled my knees just an hour before. For a few minutes, I talked about singing, about songs, about myself, about where I was from, and about all my vast worldly travels, but none of it fazed her in the least. I had come over to introduce myself, thinking that this little country girl would be impressed with this great bass singer, and the only thing I had managed to do was shoot down my own ego. I was boring her. She couldn't have cared less that I could read music or hit lower notes than anyone else in the county. After a while, I began to feel as if she were wishing I would leave her and her friends alone. Then she turned, walked a few steps, and found someone else to visit with.

Confused and dismayed, I wondered what my next step should be. I was staring at a woman who was as beautiful as Liz Taylor or any other movie star, yet to her I must have looked like the fat half of the Abbott and Costello team. Worst of all, it didn't seem she had much of a sense of humor. I was like a rookie facing Bob Feller without a clue as to how to get to first base.

I probably would have struck out and gone back to the dugout to sulk if fate hadn't intervened. Some friends had come to see us that night, and they needed a ride home. Since there wasn't enough room in the car, I volunteered to catch a ride with someone else. Out of the blue, a man I had never met offered me a ride, and I followed him to his car. I opened the door and discovered that the woman of my dreams was riding in the same backseat to which I had been assigned. Smiling, I thanked God for answering prayers and strolled back to the plate again. I soon discovered, however, that Bob Feller was still pitching.

As we bumped along the road, I quickly found out that my vision had a name—Clara. Yet I found out very little else. The closer we got to town and the more I talked, the quieter she became. She seemed to have no interest in me at all! I soon decided that she had to be the most stuck-up person I had ever met. Yet every time I looked at her perfectly defined beauty, I also reckoned she had a very good reason to be so sold on herself. As I got out of the car that night and took one final glance at her, I wondered who the lucky guy was who had so captured her heart that she had no room in it for me.

That night I couldn't go to sleep for thinking about Clara. Her face was trapped in my head. Every song I thought of seemed to be about her. Every movie I had ever seen, she now starred in. For hours I lay awake trying to figure out how to impress her. I had to find a way to convince her that I had already decided she was the woman I wanted to marry. Yet the next morning, as the sun's rays warmed the air, I was still in the same place I had been the night before—out in the cold. I hadn't come up with a single plan to convince Clara that I was the world's most wonderful guy.

Caught up in my little dream world, I determined that I needed some fresh air to clear my thoughts and get my head back on straight, so I put on my shoes and took a walk. As I headed down the town's main drag, the morning glare caused me to turn my head toward the far side of the street. There, the sun surrounding her hair like a halo, I spotted Clara walking into the post office. It is a wonder I didn't get killed as I darted across traffic without even looking one way or the other. Oblivious to the danger, I had to get to the building in time to open the door for Clara on her way out. I made it with only a few seconds to spare.

When she came through the post office door, I tried to act surprised and casual. I mumbled something to the effect of "My goodness, aren't you the Clara who was at the church where we sang last night?"

She smiled, glanced up into my face, and nodded. Once again my knees went weak and my mind went blank. I was totally befuddled. I had no idea what to say or do next. I probably would have remained in a trance-like state holding the post office door open all day long if Clara hadn't finally said, "Hi, George."

The fact that she remembered my name not only shocked me, it brought my mind back to reality. Letting the door go without even noticing if anyone was about to come through it, I smiled. "Where are you going?" I asked.

"Just came into town to pick up the mail," she replied. I thought her sweet voice literally sang when she spoke. "Now I'm going home."

"Could I walk with you?" I inquired and wondered if the begging tone in my voice had given away too much of my true feelings.

"Are you sure it isn't out of your way?" Clara questioned.

"No," I laughed. She could have lived in Houston, Texas, and I would have figured out a reason to walk her home. Wherever she was going, I was going. It didn't matter how far, how long, or how dangerous the trip.

For the next fifteen minutes, Clara and I walked and talked. Actually, Clara mainly listened while I talked. I have no idea what I said, nor do I know if my feet even hit the ground. The entire episode was almost like a dream. I just remember suddenly being at her front door, saying good-bye, and then walking back to Arthur's house feeling better than I ever had before. The rest of the day I thought about nothing but Clara. That night I set my alarm to make sure I was up in time to catch her as she walked to the post office. But I was too excited to sleep.

For the next few weeks, I lived for those daily meetings. What I initially had read as aloofness or conceit I soon found out was shyness. She may have been the most beautiful girl in three counties, but Clara didn't have much self-confidence. She didn't think she was anything special. On the night we first met, my boldness didn't put her off as much as it scared her. She was not used to being around boys who hit so hard and fast. And she certainly wasn't used to having people think she was prettier than Liz Taylor. Yet I thought this little West Virginia teenager was not only the most beautiful, but also the brightest, cleverest, and most intuitive young woman I had ever met.

Our daily "chance" meetings often turned into hour-long outings filled with talk about our lives and our dreams. Within a few weeks, she knew my whole life story. Soon our daily walks grew into evenings spent on her porch listening to the radio through an open window or just staring at the stars that lit up the clear sky. How I loved being with her!

From the moment I saw her, Clara took first place in my life. I would even skip meals just to be with her—a fact that would have astonished my mother had she lived to see it. We never did have any fancy dates; we never went out to eat or to a show. I didn't have a car or extra spending money, so we just took walks, went on picnics, or talked on the porch. In the past I might have tried to impress girls by spending money on them and taking them to nice restaurants, but with Clara there was no need. Once we got past that awkward first meeting, our time together was better than any thrill the world offered. We simply didn't need anything or anyone else but each other.

When I had a chance to spend time with my family, I told them the baby of the Younce tribe had finally fallen in love. I described Clara in terms that left my dad's and brother's jaws hanging. She was the essence of beauty, I informed them, the most perfect of all God's creations and a woman who was wise beyond her years. I assured them that no woman who had ever walked the earth was anything like her. At first they laughed and kidded me about falling so hard and fast, but when they finally met Clara, they agreed that I had found a prize. I am sure they wondered whether I could hold her. After all, I was wondering the same.

About eight months into my tour with the Watchmen, I kissed Clara good-bye as we left for Huntington, West Virginia, to sing on a big gospel show featuring a number of name acts. We were the smallest name on the bill, and the Weatherfords were the biggest. I had heard them on the radio for years. They had two shows daily on WOWO, a 50,000-watt clear-channel station out of Indiana. This mixed duet had made the big time. Friendly, outgoing, and sincere, they encouraged everyone on the Huntington bill, making all of us feel as if we were the stars and they were just honored to be working with us.

Huntington was a great night for me. I felt as if there was nothing I couldn't do with God's help. I was so grateful that he had given me this wonderful young woman to love. Just having that love bursting from my heart made me want to sing forever. I gave it all I had that night as we warmed up the crowd for the Weatherfords. Then I stood off to the side and was wowed by this group's sound, sincerity, and style. They brought heaven down and lifted people up. Their music touched me like few things ever had!

As we packed up, I was humming a song the Weatherfords had done earlier. I just couldn't get their music out of my head. After saying good night to Earl and Lily Fern Weatherford, I watched them drive off, shook my head, and sang the song a bit louder. I was glad to be singing with the Watchmen, and I was thrilled to be going home to Clara, yet I couldn't help but wonder what it would be like to sing on a radio show that was heard in twenty states and all over Canada. I silently scolded myself for even dreaming about something that big; singing with a group like the Weatherfords was way beyond my reach and talents, even on my best night!

For the next few weeks, I sang in small churches and visited with Clara on her front porch. Strange as it sounds, I was deliriously happy, but at the same time I was also growing a bit unsatisfied and frustrated. I wanted nothing more than to ask Clara to marry me, but I knew her coal miner father would not take kindly to a man with no visible means of support getting hitched to his baby daughter. Before I asked for Clara's hand, I needed to find a paying job and a place of my own. The jobs were out there, but securing one that fit my crazy schedule seemed impossible.

Taking a job in the real world could cost me a chance at singing with the group. I was in a quandary: I wanted Clara's hand worse than anything, but I just couldn't picture myself in a world where I wasn't part of a gospel quartet. I agonized over how I could make my life, my love, and my job work. I tried every way I knew to figure out a formula and just couldn't see how it could be done. I believed the Lord had called me to be a gospel singer, but it simply didn't pay enough to support a wife and family.

I would soon find out that my human way of problem solving was too limited. I kept hoping and praying a store owner who loved gospel music would somehow find me and offer me a job with flexible hours so I could keep singing with the Watchmen. In other words, I was thinking small without ever considering that God was thinking big!

One morning while I was scanning the job advertisements in the paper, the phone rang. For a change it wasn't for Arthur or Doris. On the other end of the line was another gospel singer.

"George Younce," the voice began, "I don't know if you remember me, but we sang together a few weeks ago in Huntington. I'm Earl Weatherford."

Shocked, I replied, "Sure, I remember you. You all were great. I loved listening to you work. I just haven't been able to get it out of my head."

"That's good!" Earl exclaimed. "I am so glad that you liked us. We loved you too. We thought you were one of the best young bass singers we had ever heard."

"Thank you, sir," I gasped, surprised that the Weatherfords had even listened to us sing.

"I'll tell you why I am calling you, George," Earl continued. "Our bass singer has gotten an opportunity to go home to California. He misses home, and I don't blame him for taking this chance to get back there. But it kind of leaves us in the lurch. We have to have a bass singer to get the sound we need. When we started to talk about who we could find to replace our man, we immediately thought of you."

For a few seconds I didn't say a word; I just let the offer sink in. This quartet wanted me so badly that they weren't even asking me to audition. *How could this have happened?* I wondered. Then it hit me. Once again God had put me in the right place at the right time and in the process had answered both my needs and my prayers.

Over the course of the next few minutes, Earl offered me not only a job, but more money than I knew how to spend. He also told me that he wanted me to come to Indiana on the next available bus.

That night I got together with the Watchmen and broke the news. Each of them encouraged me to go for it. If I could live my dream of singing in the big time, they felt that a part of them had made it also. Mason Lilly even loaned me enough money for a bus ticket, some clothes, and food.

As soon as I had shared the news with the guys, I rushed over to talk to Clara. Glad for what it would mean for my career, she wondered whether I would get so far away that I would forget her. I assured her that I wouldn't, and I let her know that as soon as I had a place of my own and enough money, I was going to come back for her too.

Things went by so fast that I barely had time to pack and say good-bye before I was boarding a bus headed north. As we pulled out of the station and Clara waved good-bye, it suddenly hit me that I had no idea what was in store on the other end of my journey. I wondered whether I had the talent to work with a group as good as the Weatherfords. Yet what I did have was faith. Enough seemingly unrelated events had already come together in my life to assure me that this chance was not some random act. I could feel God's hand in it and could recognize where his hand had directed me a dozen other times along the way. As I watched Clara and West Virginia fade behind me, I was confident that God was at work making my dreams come true. But just to be safe, I asked him to make sure that no good-looking boys spotted Clara until I had the chance to come back.

chapter seven

LEARNING TO BE A PRO

As the countryside rolled by, I was reminded of another long bus trip, the one that had taken me to the Stamps-Baxter school in Dallas. That seemed almost like it was in another life, yet without it I never would have taken this bus trip. Once again everything was tied together, even my emotions. Just as before, I was nervous, instantly homesick, and wondering what business I had making a move like this one. After all, the Weatherfords were not only stars of their own daily radio shows, they sold records by the boxload, and they wore nice clothes, played big churches or auditoriums, and, at least in my mind, were incapable of making mistakes. Who was I? A hick who could read an uncomplicated bass line and who had seemingly stumbled into every opportunity he had ever been given.

When my bus finally pulled into Fort Wayne, I was tired, scared, and hungry. I had been riding for almost a day, I had slept very little, and I had been too nervous to eat much. Before I got off the bus, I scanned the crowd in the old depot for anything resembling a friendly face. I saw mothers, fathers, and relatives of the passengers who had sat around me, but I couldn't pick out anyone from the Weatherfords. *What if they had forgotten about me or thought I was coming on a later bus? What would I do then? Who would I call?* I didn't know anyone!

Rising from my seat, I shuffled along the aisle behind the others, occasionally dipping down to steal a look out of the bus's side windows. Each time I stared out into the night, I saw no one waiting for me.

But when I finally stepped off the Greyhound, I noticed a great big man, over six feet tall and weighing more than two hundred fifty pounds, happily pushing his way through the crowd toward me. As soon as he spotted me, his face lit up like a Christmas tree and his smile broadened and seemed to dip down to the bottom of every one of his three chins. Dressed in a dark suit, white shirt, and tie, Earl Weatherford was a sight for sore eyes. And as he roared out "Hello, Country Boy!" and grabbed my right hand in his big mitt, my fears immediately fled. I could tell by his greeting that this man wanted me here and believed that I was the right guy for the job!

Over the next few months, I would realize that once again God had placed me in the hands of the right people to shape my life and my faith. Lily Weatherford was the sweetest woman I had known since my own mother. She was strong, fearless, and compassionate, and she knew how to encourage me. She was warm and kind and as much a mother as a member of the quartet of which I was now a member. She believed in me, and I could feel my self-confidence returning.

Earl was equally warm, but he was not as much a father as he was a teacher and coach. He worked with me, pushed me, and challenged me. He believed so strongly in my ability that he wouldn't let me rest until I had given all I had. It was through Earl's example that I would come to realize that giving everything when I sang was exactly what God had always wanted from me. He wanted my best each night, each day, and each time I performed one of his songs. Thanks to Earl, this fact became part of my professional philosophy. The one thing the Weatherfords couldn't develop as quickly as they did my musical potential, however, was my maturity. If they could have, I would have been spared a lot of growing pains and a lot of eating crow.

On my first night in Fort Wayne I was dog tired but too excited to sleep. I was alone with my doubts and wondering if too much was being expected of me. I was especially concerned that Earl expected me to be as professional as he was. I was convinced that I would fall on my face as soon as they flashed the first unfamiliar piece of music in front of me. Would the Weatherfords then figure they had made a mistake and put me on the first bus back to West Virginia?

Because I couldn't sleep, I decided to write Clara a letter. This solitary act, meant to fill a lonely night, began a habit that I continued for more than six months. Each day I would find a few spare moments and jot down everything that was on my heart, and each day I would receive a long letter in response.

Had it not been for Clara's letters and the pictures of her that filled my room, I'm not sure I would have been able to cope. She wasn't just someone I loved, but someone who was as much a part of me as were my own arms or my voice. I took her with me everywhere I went. When I sang, it was for her. And whenever I heard a love song, I thought of her. Her image haunted me, but it was a sweet haunting, one filled with a love that distance couldn't injure or kill.

My first letter to Clara was an anxious one, but my second was a lot more upbeat. As I walked into WOWO for the first time, I was overwhelmed. I had never seen a radio station so big! There were studios at every corner, and the tower was so tall it almost touched the clouds.

I knew from personal experience how far the station's signal reached. I had listened to WOWO back home in the middle of the day. At night listeners tuned in from as far away as Florida and Texas. In an era before network and cable television, this clear-channel station was bringing the world together instantly.

Jay Gould, a station manager, was one of the first to greet me as I walked in the front door. After he shook my hand and bragged about me to the employees who were wandering the halls, he gave me a tour. Then he shocked me by presenting me with a key to the front door. Because the Weatherfords had an early morning show, I would be arriving before the station's doors were unlocked. This would be my home away from home, and Jay told me that I needed to feel as if I owned the place.

I was on top of the world! I had never even had a key to the little radio station in Lenoir. As proud as I was to get a key, I still wondered if I could make a go of it as a singer. Flocks of butterflies flying in every possible direction filled my stomach before my first few rehearsals. But as soon as I started to sing, I calmed down. Danny Koker, Lily Fern, and Earl not only helped me find my notes, but they also helped me find niches in the music that exposed my talents and voice. By our third practice, they had made me feel like a member of their family. And with listeners in twenty-two states, I was soon to find out that this was a very large family indeed.

After a few more rehearsals, I was deemed air worthy. As I unlocked the door to the station on that morning, the doubts rushed back in along with the realization that Clara, my father, and the rest of my friends and family would be able to turn on their radio and hear me singing.

At 8:15, when the Weatherfords went on the air, I took a deep breath and prayed that God would somehow keep me from sounding like Daffy Duck. Miraculously, he did. When Earl asked for the "country boy" to come in close to the microphone for a featured number, I not only made it through the song, I actually thought I sounded pretty good. Later I found out that a lot of people back home did too.

As electrical inspector for the city of Lenoir, Dad had an office in the fire station. Every morning he and the firemen would gather around the station's radio, sip their coffee, and listen to the Weatherfords. Though he never said a word, the men told me that whenever he heard my voice, he smiled and a sparkle filled his eye.

Another smile lit up Clara's face in West Virginia as she sat in front of the radio, my latest letters in her hand, and "watched" me perform. Across town Jimmy and Doris also took a break to listen to "Uncle George." And at a busy car lot, Arthur Herald stopped business each day to catch his "discovery" warbling out a new tune. Overnight, just by singing a few songs, I had become a hometown hero.

With shows at 8:15 and 10:15, Monday through Friday, I got a lot of exposure. Within a week of going on the air, I received mail from twenty different states. I couldn't believe how many listeners wanted to know where they could purchase one of my records or if I could send them an autographed photo. I was a star, and I soon discovered that Earl and the station wanted to capitalize on my new identity.

Almost before I had unpacked my bags, I was in the studio cutting records with the group. Just as quickly I was shipped to the town's best clothing stores to be fitted for several nice suits and shirts. When the outfits were ready, I was whisked off for publicity photos. I had never imagined anything like this happening to me. For a while I even thought I was as high and mighty as Eddy Arnold, Red Foley, or some other big country music recording star.

Weekends on the road were even better. Earl had a seven-passenger Cadillac limo that delivered us to our dates. I had never ridden in anything so powerful, quiet, and smooth. And in every small town we drove through, people would point at the car in wonder and admiration.

I couldn't help remembering my lowly days as a busboy at Mayview Manor. I had thought that people who rode around the country in expensive cars were among the world's elite. But here I was, a country boy from North Carolina who sang bass for a gospel quartet, sitting in a Cadillac. It must be that those people at the manor weren't quiet as far up the social ladder as I had once figured. Even if they had been, I now wouldn't have traded places with them for anything in their fancy world.

No doubt my head was filled with pride during my first months with the Weatherfords. I was only twenty-four and pretty impressionable, and I was wearing expensive suits and opening bags of fan mail. There to keep me steady and focused on what the Lord had given me was Clara.

Clara's daily letters reminded me that she was in love with a country boy from a small town. The George who traveled in style might be fine for the stage, but she was stuck on the fellow who sat on the porch and wished on stars. That's the man I wanted to stay in touch with too. But as fast as things were happening, it was often hard to resist the lure of success and fame.

Earl convinced me to do some solo work. He even sent me into a recording session to cut a few sides of me singing by myself. During my first stab at this solitary approach to performing, I recorded "Amazing Grace" and "There Is a God Somewhere." About a week later I received a few boxes of "78s" on the Country Boy label. Earl always referred to me as the "country boy," so this became both my stage handle and my recording label.

Earl suggested that I sell the records at road shows and over the air at the station to make some extra money. The first thing I did, however, was ship several records back home as gifts for the Watchmen, Clara, and my family. I couldn't wait for them to hear my first solo efforts since the time I had won the prize for having the highest voice in the sixth grade.

My sister, Ruby, was a special fan. She didn't just listen to my versions of those two songs, she got inside them and used them like some people would a devotional reading. I had touched her deeply, yet at the time I wasn't even aware of what I was doing. Actually, *unaware* is a good description of me during most of this time. I was just reacting, doing whatever I was told, and basking in the afterglow when it turned out well.

The millions who listened to us each day were not as attentive or as sold on my solo career as was my sister. Even Clara liked my work with the group better than my individual efforts. But those who purchased my Country Boy records helped me make a major dream come true, one that had nothing to do with music. By banking my salary and the money I made from the records, I put away enough cash to make Clara my bride. Now all I needed was a few days off and a line of talk that would convince her father that I was worthy of his beautiful daughter.

It took eight full months for everything to come together. We had just finished singing in Toledo, Ohio, and had three days off. Waving good-bye to the Weatherfords, I caught the first train back to West Virginia. It was spring, the dogwoods were blooming, the fields were alive with wildflowers, and a special freshness filled the air—yet I barely noticed. I was of a single-minded bent. I was going to ask Clara to elope and join me back in Fort Wayne.

It was early Monday when my train rolled into town. Clara and I spent the day catching up and planning a new life together. But we couldn't make our plans a reality until I talked with her father. I had never dreaded anything more in my life.

A coal miner who spent his days in a shaft just eighteen inches high, lying on his side digging out the stuff that kept American industry going, Clara's dad was a tough man. That evening after he had cleaned up and we had eaten, I cornered him on the front porch. My voice shaking, I told him of my plans, how solid my job was, and how I loved Clara more than I could love anyone. He listened quietly as I made my case. The silence became awkward as he looked into my eyes studying me. Then he leaned toward me, and in a firm voice asked, "George, will you be good to her? Will you take care of her?"

"Sir," I responded, "I will be good to her and care for her the best I can."

"Then," he answered, "you may marry her with my blessing."

On Tuesday, April 27, 1955, Clara and I traveled over to Raven Cliff, West Virginia, and I paid three dollars for a license. As the preacher performed the ceremony, my knees grew weak. I felt as I had the first night Clara and I met. Only this time Clara didn't turn away from me. She spoke her "I do," and my life began anew.

After a one-night honeymoon in Oceania, we caught the train back to Fort Wayne and booked a room in the old Franklin Hotel. That would be our home for the next few months. These were the brightest and happiest moments I had ever known. I was convinced that I had everything a man could want.

Sometimes when life is going along smoothly, we can fool ourselves into thinking we are in a rut. In the summer of 1955, I had money in the bank, a wonderful career in radio, a wife who loved me, and time on my hands to enjoy my new bride. So what was I dreaming about? Something better, naturally.

Out of the blue I got a call from the Homeland Harmony Quartet. They were based in Atlanta, the middle of the Bible Belt and the very heart of southern gospel music. Their offer sounded good. The group worked a lot of dates, was well known in the South, and needed a solid bass singer. Without doing much thinking, I told Homeland that I would move to Atlanta as quickly as I could pack. In an action that showed I had a mature bass voice but not much real maturity, I walked away from the Weatherfords, WOWO, and Indiana.

In Atlanta, Clara and I quickly found a little apartment. I didn't have a chance to help my bride unpack. Before we got settled, I hit the road. Over the next three months, I was gone more than I was with Clara. Homesick, worn out, and completely humbled, I finally came in after an eleven-day road trip and collapsed on the bed in a state of severe depression. Clara tried to comfort me, but I could see in her eyes that she was as miserable as I was. She wasn't going to complain, but she knew that I had screwed up. I had taken the job with Homeland with no thought or prayer. I had never even considered asking the Lord if this was what he wanted. The move was my doing as well as my undoing, and now I had learned for sure that I didn't do too well on my own. It hurt me to admit that to Clara, but it was even harder to admit it to God.

In Fort Wayne we had lived the good life. We weren't rich, but we did have enough money to go out to eat and watch a movie when we wanted. Now, even though I was working all the time, all we had was thirty-four dollars. Sitting on the edge of the bed, I asked for mercy and prayed that the Lord would give me a way out of the mess I had gotten myself into. Yet even as I prayed, I didn't expect an answer anytime soon. Nor did I believe I deserved one.

Five minutes after I had finished humbling myself, the phone rang. On the other end of the line was Guy Harris, the manager of WOWO.

"George," he began, "how are you doing?"

"Not well at all," I admitted.

"Things here aren't good either," Guy informed me. "As a matter of fact, Earl needs you badly. He wanted to call you a hundred times, but you know how Earl is—he just has too much pride to do it. He wants you back. Do you want to come back?"

I could feel my throat tightening as I tried to answer Guy's question. "Yes, I want to come back, but I can't believe Earl would want me."

"I'll tell you what," Guy replied, "you stay put, and I'll see if I can get Earl to ask you himself."

I only had to wait two minutes for Earl to call, but those were the two longest minutes of my life. I felt like a prisoner on death row watching the clock tick down, all the while praying for a pardon. As I stared at the phone, I wondered if my pardon was going to come.

When the phone finally rang, I grabbed the receiver instantly. Earl must have known how excited I was by my almost breathless greeting.

"Hello."

"George, this is Earl Weatherford. I want you to come home. I need you right now, and I have even found a mobile home for you and Clara to live in. I am not going to beg, but I am sincerely asking you if you will come back to the group."

Earl didn't have to wait for my answer. I told him we were on our way. Then I called Homeland and resigned. Within minutes, Clara and I were packing. Within days, we were back home again in Indiana. When I stepped back into the radio station, I felt like the prodigal who had returned, and I was welcomed in much the same way too!

For the next few months, I gladly existed in my rut. I was happy to be where I was and wasn't looking to go anywhere else. Then the bottom dropped out. Strangely, this time things fell apart because of good news. Our ratings at WOWO had gone through the roof. The station was convinced that they needed to have more of the Weatherfords on the air each day. Management came to Earl with an all but blank check in hand and the chance to do two more shows. There was only one catch: WOWO expected us to sing popular songs on the new programs.

Earl was aghast. He felt he had been called to do gospel music, not secular music. He turned down the new shows without even considering the money he was giving up. WOWO then decided to turn up the heat, figuring that Earl would melt under the pressure. The station told our leader that if we didn't add the two pop music shows, they would simply let us go. It was all or nothing. I wasn't surprised when Earl chose nothing.

Earl's integrity might have cost him a huge radio gig, but it won him rave reviews from people of faith. One of those, a young pastor with a growing ministry in Ohio, called us up. Rex Humbard wanted to use the Weatherfords as his featured worship service singers at Calvary Temple in Akron. Within weeks of quitting WOWO, we had moved to Ohio and were performing on Sundays and Wednesdays with one of the most dynamic preachers I had ever heard.

If Clara and I had suffered any apprehension about the move, that quickly disappeared when Rex and his wife, Maude Aimee, asked us to live with them until we could find a place of our own. The Humbards were wonderful people, and they treated Clara and I as both friends and family. We never lacked anything when we were with them.

It was much the same at Calvary Temple. The church Rex was leading was a thriving, vibrant congregation who freely exhibited love and friendship. Even though the membership was ten times what it had been in the tiny Baptist church in which I had grown up, this place had a small-church feel. Coupled with this caring atmosphere was the excitement that came about when so many people with so much talent and drive banded together. The cathedral was very much like a fire that was constantly being fed more and more wood. I thrived in it!

It had been years since I had been able to be a regular part of a church. My time in the service and then singing with the Watchmen and the Weatherfords had kept me away from Sunday school, worship service, Bible studies, and prayer meetings. Now that we sang for Wednesday and Sunday services, I could get involved in both Bible study and church fellowship. For the first time in years, I was growing as a member of a larger Christian family. Clara and I began to grow our own family as well.

I was thrilled that I was going to be a father. My experience with little Jimmy Herald had convinced me that fathering wouldn't be easy, but the thought of teaching my child to play ball, sing, read, and live out all the dreams so important to a child's life had me more excited than ever. Supporting a growing family, however, meant that I needed more money. That's why I was delighted to hear that Earl had arranged another steady gig for us that would run right along with Rex's church.

Winona Lake, Indiana, was home to a small college and a radio station. The president of the college hired us to come up to a lake resort during the week and sing in an airplane he had recently purchased. He wanted to develop a show called *Wings of the Morning*. The plan was to do the show as the plane flew over the various communities the radio station served. He figured that broadcasting from the air would bring great publicity for the college and create an enrollment blitz for the next semester.

For several months Earl, Lily Fern, Danny Koker, Jim Hammel, and I did daily shows from the plane. But because of technical difficulties, the plane was anchored to the ground. Finally, when the station figured they had everything ironed out, we left the earth on what could best be described as "a wing and a prayer." At just the right moment, we got the signal and began our show. We made a big deal out of singing while aloft and included a number of songs with a heaven-bound theme. Finally, we signed off and came back down to earth, all the while figuring we would be greeted by a host of the press and fans who had been impressed by our technological feat. But except for a maintenance man, the airstrip was vacant. It hadn't worked. No one had heard anything.

As soon as we landed, the checks disappeared—we were canceled. So we went back to living in Akron and supplying the music for Rex's services. For the first time in months, things just didn't seem right. As it turned out, Danny and Jim were not getting along with Earl. I never did find out what the row was over; I only knew that it was getting worse as time dragged on. The friction that had developed between the parties began to affect our performances as well. It was now much harder to act like a family onstage.

For a while, I thought that I was a neutral third party, but because of my close friendship with Danny and Jim, Earl seemed to link me with them. Hence, when Danny and Jim decided to quit and go to work for a preacher in Milwaukee, I felt as if I had to join them too. I didn't think Earl wanted me around anymore. I left the Weatherfords for the second time, and this time there would be no coming back.

I knew nothing about Reverend Valdez and his work. Danny informed me that Valdez had a highly rated radio ministry and a growing congregation. He also pointed out that the money I would be getting would come in handy with a new baby on the way. Once I got to Milwaukee, I discovered that the fields were not even as green as they had been when I had jumped ship to sing with the Homeland Harmony Quartet in Atlanta. It was obvious from the first day that the move had been a tragic mistake. Nothing went right. All Clara and I could find was a one-room apartment where the bed pulled out of the wall. It was cold, damp, and depressing.

Danny, Jim, and I were also having problems putting together a quartet. We simply couldn't find anybody to sing with us. Everyone we tried fell through within a week or two of joining us. At one point, we discovered a guy who we thought had the greatest voice we had ever heard. We signed him after hearing him sing just one solo. The only problem was, that song was the only one he could sing. Within two days he was on his way home too.

Day after day, week after week, the guys and I struggled along. We told ourselves there were better days ahead, but none of us really believed it. We could sense the wheels coming off our wagon; the only question left was which one of us was going to step forward and give up first. As the November winds blew in, my moods were often as gray as the lakefront clouds.

Just when I figured things couldn't get worse, Danny got drafted. It was December, and Christmas was only a week away. I told Jim that without Danny I just didn't feel like going on. He agreed. Phoning home, I alerted my family that Clara and I would be joining them for the holidays. Then we packed, loaded what we owned in our old car, and headed toward North Carolina.

Before I had left Milwaukee, I had made a couple of calls. One of them had been to Philadelphia. Urias Le Fevre and his family were singing in a big church there. They also had a radio show. I had met Mr. Le Fevre when I had been with the Weatherfords. He told me then to let him know if I ever decided to move to another group. True to his word, Urias invited me to come on up after Christmas and he would put me to work. Though I knew this new job wouldn't be as financially rewarding as the one I formerly had with the Weatherfords, at least I could celebrate Christmas with the knowledge that I could stay in gospel music, sing with some good people, and feed my family. That seemed like a pretty big answered prayer to me. What I would soon be reminded of was that my thinking was again much smaller than God's.

chapter eight

SINGING IN THE BLUE RIDGE

As Clara and I drove home, I spent a lot of time thinking. Even though I had a tremendous amount of respect for Urias Le Fevre, I questioned whether I was taking a spot with him because I needed the money or because the Lord had called me there. After my experience in Milwaukee, I needed to feel God in my actions. I didn't want to do anything else on impulse.

Overwhelmed by my own doubts and in need of the reassurance that I was indeed doing the right thing, I stopped in Wheeling, West Virginia, to call an old friend, Ace Richmond. Ace had been in the gospel music business for a long time, and he knew things from top to bottom. If he told me to take the job and head north after Christmas, I would feel it was a part of the master plan. When I opened the door to that West Virginia pay phone, I really believed God was leading me to call this man who now sang with the Sunshine Boys.

Gospel music was and still is a big business in a small world. Though there were a thousand quartets at that time, when anything happened to one of them, the word got out in a hurry. It still works that way today. So it wasn't surprising that even before Ace answered the phone, he knew what had happened in Milwaukee.

"Tough luck," Ace told me as we talked, "but I find that things usually happen for the best."

At that point I didn't see much good in what was happening. I was about to start a family, had lost a lot of money as well as respect during my few months in Wisconsin, and was broke. I wanted to believe that things were headed in the right direction, so I agreed with the veteran performer.

"George," Ace assured me, "you have a lot of talent. You are a good singer. There will always be a place for you in this business. Just pray a bit and keep the faith. When the time comes, you will know that the Lord is right there with you."

A little disappointed, I thanked Ace, hung up, and headed back to the car and Clara. His words just didn't offer the assurance I was hoping for. I needed him to tell me to take the job. He didn't. I needed him to assure me to push forward. He didn't. All he did was tell me to keep the faith—or at least that was all I thought he did.

What I didn't know was that as soon as we had ended our phone conversation, he had placed a long-distance call to Elmo Fagg. Elmo, who was with the Blue Ridge Quartet, had heard me perform when I was just seventeen years old. Elmo remembered me from my Spiritualaires days, and as Ace told him about my situation, the Blue Ridge leader wanted to know just how firm my commitment was to the Le Fevres. It seemed he needed a bass singer.

I had no more walked into my father's home in Lenoir, exchanged a few handshakes and hugs, when the phone rang. My father answered, spoke for a few seconds, then yelled across the room for me to come to the receiver. I hadn't been home long enough for anyone to know that I was there. I was shocked when I found out that Elmo Fagg was on the other end of the line.

"George," he began, "Ace Richmond called me and filled me in on what happened. That mess up in Milwaukee was a real shame for you and your friends, but it might just be an answered prayer for me. You see, I've lost my bass singer. I have to have one right now. I was wondering if you could come up to Spartanburg and try out with us. If my mind, my heart, and my memory aren't fooling me, I think that you are just the man we need for the job."

I was astounded! I couldn't believe that the Blue Ridge Quartet, the very same group that I had raced home from the furniture factory to hear on the radio each day, would be interested in me. As soon as I could, I rushed to Spartanburg to display my wares.

After Elmo introduced me to the other members of the group, Kenny Gates and Ed Spraus, we all drank a Coke and discussed music for a few minutes. Then, when it appeared that everyone was comfortable, we looked through an old songbook to find some things we all knew. We eventually agreed on a couple of old standards and launched into them to find out if our voices would mesh. As we finished the second song, I was about to suggest a couple more that might better suit my voice and style, but I didn't get the chance. It seemed that Elmo had already gotten the thumbs up from Kenny and Ed. Judged on just five minutes of work, I had been given the job. What a Christmas present!

I bowed my head and silently said a short and jubilant prayer. This time I did feel the Lord's hand in the offer. Assured that I was where God wanted me to be, I vigorously shook hands with each of the three guys and raced out to the phone to call Clara.

Urias Le Fevre was the next person on my list. When I told him of my latest offer, he encouraged me to go for it. I don't think Urias really needed me at that point; rather, he found a place for me because he was making good on a longtime promise. He was probably relieved that someone else needed me. Thus, getting him to let me go was no problem at all.

After a wonderful Christmas with our families, Clara and I moved to Spartanburg and set up house. With a baby on the way and my career back on track, things couldn't have been better. From the start, I really got along well with Elmo, Kenny, and Ed; and even though we had to travel more than I wanted, I felt ready to be a father.

It was a cool day in May when Gina was born, but it was my warmest day since I had married my wife. Our baby was beautiful. Sure, she looked just about like the rest of the little ones lying in the cribs at the hospital, but I thought she stood out. There was a sparkle in her eye that seemed to indicate she was more intelligent than the little ones on either side of her. And the way she wrapped her fingers around mine when I held her told me she was stronger than any child who had ever been born. I thought she looked like Clara, which also made her more beautiful than any child had a right to be. She was absolutely perfect—until we got her home. That was when I discovered that while she got her looks from Clara, she got her lungs from her daddy. She was loud, demanding, and performed often. I had never realized just how annoying crying could be.

When I was at home, I held my daughter, played with her, made faces over her, and, of course, sang to her. When she cried, I worried, and each night I prayed that God would help me take care of her. When I was on the road, I missed her terribly.

Brudge would come up and take Clara and Gina home to stay with his family whenever I left for a long tour. It was comforting to know that not only did Clara have help, but that Gina was getting to know my family in a very intimate way. Because of performers' hectic schedules, many simply never get to share special relationships with their children. The fact that my brother made this possible for me not only enhanced my life but my children's lives as well. In a sense, he became a second father, the man who could step in when I wasn't there. This gave me great peace when I was on the road.

Along Tobacco Row in the fifties the Blue Ridge Quartet were stars. We not only worked high school gyms and small-town theaters, but we also cut records and had our own television show on the local Spartanburg station. The program was sponsored by Coca-Cola, which meant that we always had something to drink on the road and at home too. Coke and the Blue Ridge Quartet were "the real thing"—at least to me. I couldn't begin to repay either one for all they meant in my life.

Hundreds of wonderful things came out of those years. The memories, largely personal and not very interesting, are still vivid in my mind. They include concerts, jokes, prayer times, my growth as a singer (thanks to the influence of the other quartet members), and of course the thousands of fans I came to know more on a friendship level than as entertainer to audience. These were more precious than any material gift anyone could have given me, and I did my best to give some of these gifts back in kind. Two very special gifts came through Elmo Fagg, gifts that I simply couldn't put a value on or pay back.

When Elmo invited me to join the Blue Ridge Quartet, he allowed me to settle down and establish roots for the first time. Clara and I bought a nice brick home, joined a church, made friends, and became a part of the community. All these things, coupled with two more "perfect" daughters, Dana and Lisa, helped me mature as I never had before. In the past I had turned to God when things became rough or when I thought I needed a miracle; now, as the blessings multiplied around me, I turned to him every day. For the first time, I wasn't asking as much as I was thanking.

Spartanburg was where I learned to tithe. It was also where I learned what it meant to not only sing for Christ, but to live for him too. I studied the Bible and searched for ways to serve God outside of music and to be a good role model for my children and my wife. At many points, I might not have measured up to the rock I strove to be, but I think I succeeded a bit in the role model area simply because I tried so hard to be a good husband and daddy.

Dana and Lisa were every bit as beautiful as Gina. Like her, they always knew exactly how to get whatever they wanted from me. I blame Gina for this. When she came along, I was innocent and igno-rant. I didn't know how to say no and didn't realize that an infant was capable of controlling me. Gina must have passed along her secrets to her two sisters, because I soon discovered that they were as good at it as she was. By and large, I think all three of them were just smarter than I was from the get-go. Their intelligence must have come from Clara, but once again, children number two and three got their voices from me.

The second invaluable gift that I received from Elmo Fagg involved learning how to work a crowd. Elmo was a master at keep-ing people interested in what we were doing. Whether on television or at a live show, he was in control. He knew when to lighten up, and he also sensed when it was time to speak from the heart. He knew when to be a ham and entertain, but he also knew when to be seri-ous and lead people to worship through our music. While I loved watching him work and I enjoyed chiming in from time to time, it never dawned on me that someday I would be a master of ceremonies for a gospel group. Back then, when Elmo was ill and I was forced to step into that job, I dreaded it. Yet by watching him, I learned not only to sing, but to read the crowd and learn what they wanted and needed. Through his influence, I realized that giving the audience your heart and music wasn't enough, you had to bring smiles and tears too. You had to touch them spiritually rather than just enter-tain them.

Elmo was good at this because he wasn't trying to be anything but what he was. He didn't put on. He wasn't fake. It didn't take long for me to learn that people wanted to know the real person. They didn't want a pumped-up image of what a gospel singer was supposed to be; they wanted to see the warts and all—straightforward and honest. If they liked what they saw, they'd want to come back again and again.

So these were the best learning years of my life, and I owe most of that to Elmo and my wife and daughters.

When I wasn't racing around our house chasing kids, I was racing out on a stage somewhere. Out of our television show sprang a syndicated gospel hour that was seen all over the country. *The Gospel Singing Caravan* assembled some great talent. Along with the Blue Ridge Quartet, there were the Le Fevres, the Johnson Sisters, and the Prophets. The show was sponsored by Martha White Flour, and within weeks of going on the air, our bookings went through the roof.

From the start, we hoped this show would expose us to a larger audience, but we didn't really grasp just how much our fan base was going to grow. As we rolled into the small towns where we were playing, we began to note sold-out signs hanging in theater windows and people lined up in the morning to get tickets for that night. For guys who were used to singing for crowds that rarely numbered more than a few hundred, this seemed like the big time.

What we experienced could be explained at least in part by the expanding power of television. The visual impact of seeing us sing on that black and white tube was greater than hearing us on radio. The fact that most viewers in the Bible Belt received only one or two stations also gave us an advantage. If we were on the air, we were often the only choice viewers had, so they got to know us well.

Another influence on our increasing popularity was a strong economy. For the first time ever, I watched family after family arrive at our shows in new Fords and Chevrolets. Earlier crowds had been forced to scrimp and save just to buy quarter tickets; now our audiences were arriving in style and even had pocket change for records.

Music of all kinds was exploding across the nation at this time. Country music had grown like gangbusters, and Nashville was a mecca for new stars. Rock and roll had sprung to life and had taken over a good part of the airwaves. Rhythm and blues also was being accepted in the mainstream. Music had become more important in America than ever before, and it was also more commercially successful than at any time in history. Not only were kids with ducktails and guitars benefiting, we were too.

Initially, with Ed Spraus as tenor, Elmo had built our quartet into an ensemble as good as any in the country at that time. Our harmonies were solid, we worked hard during rehearsals, and we gave people what they wanted—a combination of new gospel songs coupled with the old standards. With Kenny Gates hitting between the ivories on piano, we were a group that could shape a song and tell a story.

By 1957 we were on a roll. I had emerged from poverty and joined the middle class, with a home and a nice car to prove it. Hence, when I arrived at the National Quartet Convention in Memphis, Tennessee, I was confident and ready to sing on a program featuring the greatest gospel music stars ever assembled. That is how deep my belief was in myself and the four guys who worked at my side.

When I strolled in that evening, I noted that one of the dressing rooms seemed filled with a few more people than normal. I didn't have time to pay much attention to the group that had gathered and was harmonizing in a corner. I was focused on my own job. Yet as the strains of "Walk Them Golden Stairs" emerged from the room, I found myself wanting to make a sharp U-turn and join in the old song. Though I didn't know it then, I would soon get my chance.

A few minutes later, after we had begun singing "Child of the King," I noticed a young man seated backstage just out of view of the audience. As I sang my part, I observed him singing along note for note. He had me down pat. The bright spotlight shining in my face, coupled with the shadows surrounding the man offstage kept me from seeing his face. Yet as his foot bounced and his head moved, I could tell he was really getting into the spirit of the song. As our segment of the show moved on, I grew more intent on working the audience and focused less of my attention on the mystery gospel music fan seated to my left. When we concluded our set and I turned to walk offstage, he was still there. Only this time he was standing and applauding even more vigorously than the thousands in front of the stage.

When the curtain fully closed, the young man rushed up to me. I could tell by his mannerisms that he was obviously excited by the prospect of meeting the bass singer of the Blue Ridge Quartet.

Extending his hand, he smiled a smile that would have lit the whole room. "I love your range, sir," he said. "The way ya'll do 'Child of the King' is incredible."

As I shook the good-looking young man's hand, I suddenly realized who he was. It was hard to believe that the hottest name in entertainment history was spending his night huddled backstage listening to gospel quartets. Yet as I was soon to discover, Elvis Presley had the night off not by accident, but because he wouldn't allow anyone to book him during the quartet convention. In the rocker's mind, this was the best place on earth.

I followed Elvis back to a dressing room, where we were soon joined by a half dozen other guys. With the King of Rock and Roll urging us on, we began to sing standards all of us had learned as children. Elvis, who seemed captivated with the bass parts, would then join in. These impromptu sessions, broken up only when Presley rushed to his seat just offstage to catch a particular act he loved, went on until the convention closed for the evening. It was the best "singing" I had ever attended. Someone would say, "Hey, do you remember this one?" and off we'd go.

When everyone started to pack up and head out the back door, I thought it was over. Yet when I was walking toward the car Elvis called to me.

"Mr. Younce, sir," his voice eager and full of life, "I've asked some of the guys to come back to Graceland to sing around my piano. We'll have food and soft drinks there, and I would be honored if you would join us. I guarantee we are going to have a lot of fun."

The invitation sounded great, and I assured Elvis that I would try to make it. Singing at Graceland sure beat staying in a hotel room by myself. David Reese of the Harvesters had been invited too, and he offered to drive me over to Presley's home. But neither of us knew how to get around in Memphis, let alone where Graceland was located. We spent three hours driving in circles until we gave up and headed back to the hotel. It was three in the morning, and we were sure that even if we found the place, everybody already would have gone home. The next day I ran into J. D. Sumner and some others who had made it to Graceland. I discovered, much to my dismay, that the singing had lasted all night long.

Even though I missed going to Graceland, through the years I saw Elvis several more times at the annual conventions. I never met a young man who was more respectful, sincere, and full of love for gospel music. A part of him came to life when he joined in on a quartet spiritual. It was like watching a bird who had been freed from a cage joyously flying through the air. His fame had trapped him and was smothering him. The more I was around him, the more my heart broke for him. I believe that Elvis's real love was gospel music. I am glad that I had a chance to visit and sing with him backstage. Through this experience I met the real Elvis Presley. I am only sorry that the real Elvis couldn't have enjoyed life the way he should have.

In 1958 Ford introduced the Edsel just in time for the nation's economy to fall apart. A recession hit, the Edsel flopped, our concert bookings fell off, and I became disenchanted. I was a middle-class family man who was used to having a cushion in my checking account. When my cut of the Blue Ridge profits shrank, I began to look for greener pastures. When the Florida Boys offered me a solid monthly salary, I accepted.

I lived with my mistake for three months. I wasn't happy, and once again I wasn't where the Lord wanted me. Surprisingly, Elmo let the prodigal come back home, and he didn't make me crawl or beg. He even let me help establish a new set of goals for the Blue Ridge Quartet to assure us an income that would feed our families. Things didn't turn around overnight, however. We weathered the bad times for over a year, then in 1960 things once again headed in the right direction.

For the next four years, we toured, developed our television show, and cut more albums. We were blessed at every corner. Along with my Blue Ridge brothers, I was now stuck in a glorious rut that was comfortable, offered security, and had become progressively easier. I didn't figure that I would ever leave Spartanburg or the group. I was so "settled in" that I rarely even talked about openings in other quartets. I just knew that nothing short of World War III was going to make me move. Then in 1964, the phone rang.

Out of the blue my old friend Rex Humbard called me. At first we caught up on family talk. Then Rex guided our conversation to his ministry. I knew that the Weatherfords had left him and moved back to their home in Oklahoma. I was also aware that Danny Koker, Bobby Clark, and Glen Payne, vocalists with that group, had stayed in Akron and continued to sing at Rex's televised services. While the new group, known as the Cathedral Trio, was good, Rex and Glen felt they should expand into a quartet. But to do so, they needed a good solid bass. Rex wanted me to join this talented threesome.

The last thing I wanted to do was accept Rex's offer. After all, I had a beautiful house close to my childhood home, a wonderful working relationship with the guys in our quartet, fabulous friends, and a contented family. There was no way I wanted to leave Spartanburg. Yet for a reason I didn't even understand, I told Rex I would consider his offer.

That evening Clara and I discussed our options. There didn't seem to be any logic in the move. Yet as we talked and prayed and talked some more, we felt the Lord urging us on. For the first time in my life, I was almost disappointed with the Lord. The fact that he seemed to be pushing me away from a place where I was happy into an adventure that had few guarantees and a lot of unknowns bothered me. Besides, how could I leave this group after all they had done for me? Would that be a Christian thing to do?

I was deeply troubled and couldn't sleep, yet it wasn't because I didn't know the direction I was supposed to take. I knew it all right, I just didn't understand or agree with it. I wanted to stay where life was easy and comfortable. I didn't want a new challenge. Yet fight as I did, I also knew that God wasn't going to let me ignore him. I finally gave in. The next day I broke the news to Elmo and then called Rex and informed him that Clara, the girls, and I were on our way. And I still didn't know why. *Would I ever know why?* I wondered as I stepped into a future I couldn't see and never dared imagine.

PART TWO

Glen's Story

chapter nine

A YOUNG BOY'S DREAM

As a young boy working in the fields, I learned to judge the time based on the position of the sun, the gnawing hunger in my gut, the dryness in my mouth, and the number of cotton rows I had been able to hoe. By the time I was eight, my system worked so well that I knew almost to the second when it was time to lay aside my tools and race to the house for lunch. And when the dinner bell rang, race I would. I couldn't wait to get to the kitchen!

While my mother's cooking was always good, it wasn't what encouraged me to set a new sprint record every day. Something very special was waiting for me exactly at noon. I would have been crushed to have missed even a second of it.

Before I tell you what it was, take a moment and picture a ten-year-old boy dressed in old overalls racing barefoot across Texas dirt, a boy who didn't have much magic in his life. My parents, Elmer and Vela Payne, didn't have enough resources to erase the hard realities of the Depression. Never had a mother and a father worked harder to give their children everything they could with so little results. We were flat-out poor, and our neighbors, the people in the next town, and millions across the country were in the same fix.

Though as the oldest child I didn't have to wear hand-me-downs, my clothes were patched and worn. A piece of fruit or a pair of socks was all we could expect at Christmas. A bottle of soda, even though only a nickel, was the most special of treats. While homemade candy was rare, a store-bought candy bar was an unparalleled luxury.

Yet even in the midst of poverty, we had one thing most of our neighbors didn't—a radio. That radio was the instrument that brought magic into my life. It allowed me to escape, transporting me to thousands of places I had never been and enabling me to dream big, beautiful, hopeful dreams during an era when too many dreams had turned into nightmares. The radio drew me like nothing else could, not even the smell of the best home-cooked meal a boy could imagine.

The kitchen was full of the smell of pinto beans and corn bread as I rushed through the door each day. Greeted by my mother's warm voice, I hurried across the room to make sure the radio was tuned to the right station. It had to be KRLD at 1080, and the first thing I had to hear, right after the twelve o'clock time tone, was a harmonizing gospel quartet singing "Give the World a Smile." No matter how tough the morning's work had been, the Stamps Quartet and their theme song always brought a smile to me too.

V. O. Stamps, Marion Snider, and the other members of the Stamps were my heroes. The songs they sang each day were my best friends. I would take them with me as I worked the fields or walked to school. Other boys may have idolized Babe Ruth or Dizzy Dean and dreamed of playing baseball for the St. Louis Cardinals or New York Yankees, but not me. I wanted to be a singer and make people smile and feel good even in bad times. More than anything else in the world I wanted to be a member of a quartet.

As we ate lunch, Mom would have to remind me not to sing along with the radio at the table. I just couldn't help it! Not only did I sing as I ate, played, and worked, I went to sleep quietly humming gospel tunes and wondering what it would be like to sing on the radio.

By today's standards my ten-year-old dreams must seem pretty small. Yet they had to be small. I was enough of a realist to know there weren't many breaks to be had in north-central Texas. People who were poor usually had a tough, long road out. Most of the people who lived around me weren't getting too far down that road either. If you were eating regularly, you were fortunate.

I was three years old when the Depression hit and pretty much wiped out any chance the citizens of Munson, Texas, had of getting a piece of the American dream. Cotton dropping to a nickel a pound, the drought, and the exodus of hopeless country people traveling long highways to find a better life in the West had combined to kill most people's hopes and dreams. Life's daily realities were so harsh and good times so far off that those who stuck it out on the farms survived mainly on prayer and pioneer stubbornness. My parents had their share of both.

Like most farmers, my mom and dad were very determined, and they had always prayed. But they hadn't always been poor. About the time I was born, the Paynes were on the verge of making a move toward middle-class life. In 1926 there wasn't much to Munson besides a couple of grocery stores, a cotton gin, a few small homes, and one interdenominational church. My mom and dad felt that it was a good place to live, worship, and start a family.

When I was taking my first steps and learning how to put words together, a coal oil stove exploded in our home and changed our economic status in a flash. Miraculously, no one was hurt in the explosion, but we lost everything in the fire that followed. Picking up the few items they could salvage, my parents packed up their car and moved up the road to Nevada, Texas. For the next few years, an old frame house with peeling paint set beside a dirt trail would be our home. Not too long after we moved to that place, my brother and sister, Kenneth and Wanda Lee, came along and completed our little family.

As the son of a farmer who was the son of a farmer, I was grounded in the soil and understood very early the meaning of hard work. Almost from the time I could read, farm chores were a part of my life. I was used to the hot sun and long cotton rows. I knew what it was like to get up early to gather eggs and milk a cow. I also knew that it didn't do any good to complain. The work was always there, and it always had to be done. The one thing that made the work easier was the music I heard on the Stamps' broadcasts and at church.

Even after we moved up the road to Nevada, the tiny church in Munson was still our spiritual home. Inside those modest walls my family experienced some of the best times any of us can remember. There during Friday and Saturday night "singin's," as well as Sunday and Wednesday services, the Paynes came together with friends and relatives for fellowship, worship, and good times. My dad, Elmer, was the music superintendent. My Grandfather Smith, a man who for some reason I called Dad, was the Sunday school director. My mother and grandmother taught classes and led Bible studies, and all of us sang every time we had a chance.

Like so many small churches in the South and Southwest, our congregation bought our songbooks from the Stamps-Baxter Publishing

Company of Oak Cliff, Texas. This was the same company that sponsored the radio show I heard each day at noon. More than any textbook I studied at the country school, it was the well-worn shaped-note Stamps-Baxter hymnal that would provide me with the real basics I needed in life. It even offered me my first reading lessons.

For those who don't remember or were never exposed to them, shaped-note songbooks were how country people learned to read music. Each note on the scale had a different shape. Thus, when you learned what shape was *do*, what was *mi, sol, la*, and so forth, you could sing any part of any song in any key by simply reading the shape of the note. It may sound complicated, but it really was a shortcut that offered millions a chance to learn to read music.

I wasn't alone. A lot of people turned to the songs in those songbooks for comfort, wisdom, inspiration, and joy. Books like *Favorite Songs and Hymns* were filled with hymns that offered answers to any kind of need. Even as a child I remember marveling at how those wonderful songwriters could tell the stories so vividly that I not only heard them, but saw and felt them as well. Millions leaned on the messages in those hymnals to make it through the tough times. As much as those words are now etched into my life's work, I wonder what would have become of me if I had not been born to parents who treasured the Lord, his house, and his music as much as mine did.

I was blessed to have had Vela Gertude Payne as my mother. A hardworking person, she would get up before dawn to wash and cook. Then she would work in the fields even during the hottest days, rush back home to get lunch ready, then join us again for an afternoon of labor. Somehow after supper she always seemed to find the time and energy to read to us or sing along with us. And on most nights, long after I had fallen asleep, she would still be mending, sewing, cleaning, or doing a dozen other things that had to be done to make sure we had the best she could give us.

My dad was the same. I don't know when he rested. Even when he worked a farm, he sought out other odd jobs. By the time I entered fourth grade, he had gone to work at a broom factory in Rockwall, and we had moved to that small community. It wouldn't be our final move either. Thanks to the hard times and my dad's drive to give us the best he could, we would live a few more places before I grew up. He was always looking for something better for us.

In Dad and Mom's quest to give us the best, they never failed to open the door for us to grow in faith. Bible study, prayer, and church attendance were not something they just did, they were a part of everything my parents were about. These living examples of faith within my own family offered a stabilizing influence in the turmoil of the times. Therefore, moving from home to home and school to school didn't bother me. I knew that family was held together by more than living in a certain house or a certain town. We thrived even in the bad times because of love and faith. And while those were the two things that continually drove my father to push to do better, they were also the things that kept him and Mom going to church every time the doors were opened.

My grandparents were anchors for me as well. Grandpa Smith was a big man with an even bigger heart. He was one of the greatest people I had ever known. He and my grandmother, a kindly old country woman with a smile that made all the wrinkles around her eyes come together, always encouraged me to keep dreaming. While others may have laughed at the little boy who sang in the fields, these two didn't. In fact, they encouraged me to sing every chance I got, in church and at family get-togethers. They made me feel special, important, and talented.

In the spring of 1938, my grandfather somehow scraped together an extra half-dollar and gave me the most wonderful present I had ever received. With great ceremony he announced that he and I were going to go to the school in Josephine, Texas, to watch the Stamps Quartet perform live.

I couldn't believe it. This was the most exciting thing that had ever happened to me. No dream I had ever dreamed had been this big! I was actually going to see the men to whom I had been listening most of my life. I didn't want to wish for too much, but I couldn't help praying I would meet them too.

The week leading up to the concert was the longest of my life. I had problems sleeping, concentrating, and even visiting with my friends. I was excited, nervous, and a little scared.

Josephine was hardly as big as Munson. It was really not much more than a wide spot in the road. The school auditorium, the biggest room in town, probably didn't hold more than four hundred people. Yet as Grandpa and I drove up on that warm spring evening, it seemed like everyone in town was there.

Those who lined up beside my grandfather and me were mainly farmers and their wives. Most had driven up to the school in worn-out Fords or horse-drawn wagons. The tickets were twenty-five cents for adults and fifteen cents for children. Most people I knew couldn't have spared even that amount.

By arriving early, my grandfather and I were able to get seats near the small stage. I had never been to anything but church singings, so I didn't know what to expect. In front of me was a bare stage furnished with only a piano. There were no special lights or sound system. All around me were people dressed in their Sunday best, smiling and speaking in low tones.

As the seconds ticked by, I noted a slight breeze coming from the open windows on the side of the room. Outside those windows were scores of people who couldn't afford the price of admission but still wanted to hear the Stamps' music live.

As I fidgeted and continued to gaze around the room, I noted the crowd grow suddenly hushed. Looking up at the stage, I saw five nicely dressed gentlemen walk out. One, a man I knew to be Marion Snider from a church singing convention I had attended, sat down at the piano. The other four stood in a line just a few feet from the edge of the stage.

I held my breath as Marion hit the opening to "Give the World a Smile." As the quartet began their parts, their voices carrying across the auditorium, my heart raced and my mouth grew dry. Chills ran up and down my spine. I let my eyes race from man to man and back again. Under my breath I sang each note and silently whispered each word. And when the Stamps finished their theme song, I clapped so hard and smiled so big that I was sure they had noticed me. Then the show went on!

I will never forget the way those four men's voices blended as they sang "Kneel at the Cross." I actually felt transported to Calvary. I could also sense the Lord working in my heart, soul, and gut. He was alive, and I was flying! As the night rolled on and the group sang more and more of the songs I had heard on the radio, I became lost in the concert. I wasn't aware of the crowd around me, the hot room,

The Cathedrals live on the *Today* show—1995

George, Clara, Van, and Glen

George Younce and family
l to r: Rick Eroskey (son-in-law), Gina Younce-Eroskey (daughter), Terri Younce (daughter-in-law), Morgan Younce (granddaughter), George Lane Younce (son), Ernie Haase (son-in-law), Lisa Younce-Haase (daugher), Dana Younce-Willis (daughter), Clara Younce (wife), Robbie Willis (son-in-law); *center:* George Younce

Glen and Van with grand-children Marla and Jordan

Darla, Todd, and Carla, National Quartet Convention, 1994

Glen and Van's son-in-law, Bill; daughter, Carla; and grandchildren, Jordan and Marla

George's first quartet: Spiritualaires—1947
l to r: Stanley Wilson, Herb Miller, Ike Miller, George Younce, Willis Abernathy

Spiritualaires at the Stamps-Baxter School of Music in 1947
l to r: Stanley Wilson, Herb Miller, Bill Devlin,
George Younce, Bob Elmore

l to r: George's father, Tom Younce; George Younce with his puppy "Coley"; George's mother, Nellie Younce

George Younce—1950
Partroopers-82nd Airborne Division

George's wife, Clara Younce, at 16 years old (1954)

Watchmen Quartet—1954
standing l to r: Arthur
Harold, George Younce,
Mason Liffey
seated: Jack Clark

The Weatherfords—1955
top from left: George Younce, Norman Wood, Earl Weatherford
bottom from left: Lily Fern Weatherford, Danny Koker

Watchmen Quartet—1956
l to r: Jim Hamill, Tallmadge Martin, George Younce, Danny Koker

Blue Ridge Quartet—1957
clockwise from left:
George Younce, Elmo Fagg, Ed Sprouse, Kenny Gates, Bill Crowe

Munson Quartet—1939
l to r: Glen Payne (age 13), Everett Vance, Gertrude Payne (Glen's mother), Elmer Payne (Glen's father), Vernan Vance

Stamps-Baxter Quartet—1944
l to r: Loy Hooker, Glen Payne (17 years old), Curt Garner, Roger Clark, Harley Lester

Lester Stamps Quartet—1947
center row l to r: Loy Hooker, Glen Payne, Harley Lester, Austin Arnold

Stamps All Star Quartet 1948
l to r: Clyde Garver, Albert Haupe,
R. D. Ginnett, Glen Payne, Haskell Mithcell

Glen in the service

Stamps All Star Quartet—1949
standing l to r: Roger Clark, Jack Taylor, Clyde Garner, Glen Payne
seated: Haskell Mitchell

Stamps Ozark Quartet—1953
l to r: Pat Garner, Glen Payne, Livey Freeman (seated), Charles Bartlett, Fred Bennett

Nov. 30, 1958
The wedding of Glen Payne and Van Lua Harris, performed by the Reverend Rex Humberd, was the first to be televised from the Cathedral of Tomorrow. It will long be remembered as one of the largest and most beautiful ceremonies in the Akron area.

Glen's mom and dad, and Carla

Stamps Ozark Quartet—1955
clockwise from left: Pat Garner, Glen Payne, Fred Bennett, Henry Slaugheter

The Weatherfords—1957
l to r: Glen Payne, Lily Weatherford, Earl Weatherford. Armond Morales
seated: Henry Slaughter

Cathedrals Trio—1963
l to r: Glen Payne, Danny Koker, Bobby Clark

The original Cathedrals—1964
l to r: George Younce, Glen Payne, Danny Koker, Bobby Clark

The Cathdrals—1971
standing l to r: Roger Horne, Glen Payne
seated l to r: George Younce, Roy Tremble, Lorne Matthews

The Cathedrals—1973
standing: Bill Dykes, Glen Payne
seated: Roy Tremble, George Webster, George Younce

The Cathedrals—1975
standing: Glen Payne,
George Younce
seated: Haskell Cooley,
George Webster,
Roy Tremble

The Cathedrals—1979
Roy Tremble, George Webster, Glen Payne, George Younce, Lorne Mathews

The Cathedrals—1983
l to r: Kirk Talley,
George Younce,
Roger Bennett, Glen
Payne, Mark Trammell

The Cathedrals—1984
standing l to r: George Younce,
Glen Payne, Mark Trammell
seated l to r: Roger Bennett,
Danny Funderburk

The Cathedrals—1987
standing l to r: Gerald Wolfe,
Mark Trammell,
Danny Funderburk
seated l to r: George Younce,
Glen Payne

or even the passage of time. To this day I don't know if my grandfather had more fun watching me or the quartet. I know he felt that every penny he spent on that concert was worth it. All the way home I talked and sang incessantly.

Grandma was as excited as her husband when she heard what a great time I had. She had probably given up her chance to go in order for Grandpa to take me. From a lifetime of having her unconditional love, I knew that she was always sacrificing for those she loved. Only I didn't know that giving up her ticket for me would be one of her last acts of love.

A few months after the show, Grandma, without warning, got sick and died. I remember the hole in my heart as I watched the rain pour down on her funeral procession. I imagined that God himself was crying. The dear lady was buried outside of Royse City, and the roads were so muddy that the hearse got stuck a half dozen times on the way to the cemetery. Finally, a group of men, dressed in their best suits, got behind the old vehicle and pushed it up the final hill to the cemetery. Just like that road, I was grudgingly letting heaven take her. This was the first time I had ever lost someone close to me, and I didn't know how to handle it; I just knew that the world had never seen such a sad day. I didn't think I would ever get over the pain.

The next morning the sun came out and we began life again. The songs I sang in the field that day were softer and more pleading, and my faith may have been weaker too.

About the only thing that helped me deal with Grandma's death was the routine of hearing the Stamps' broadcasts each day. Their songs were like medicine. Because they had meant so much to her, they brought a piece of her to me each day. And now that I had seen the group in person and could put faces with the voices, the music that sprang from the kitchen radio even became more alive! Just when I needed them most, the words had even greater impact. This small bit of solace would soon grow into a mighty lesson that V. O. Stamps and others would teach me in person, but at that moment it was a small crutch to fit a child's need.

chapter ten

A SHAPED-NOTE
EDUCATION

IN THE FIRST WEEKS and months after my grandmother's death, I found that I missed her more deeply than I had thought possible. I simply couldn't imagine how anyone else could lift my spirits in the special way that she had. What I couldn't have known at that time was that the Lord had someone else very special out there for me and my family and that he would soon be sending her to touch me in ways no one else could.

I had known Miss Stodgill my whole life. In fact, she had helped deliver me when I was born. She was also in church each Sunday morning to pinch my cheek or tell me how much I had grown. When she would hear me at a sing-around at someone's home or at church, she would compliment me and tell me just how much talent she thought I had. I liked her because of the way she singled me out and made me feel special. As my fondness for this woman grew, I failed to notice that another member of my family was developing a deep affection for Miss Stodgill too.

When my grandmother died, Grandpa was forced to face life alone for the first time in more than three decades. I wondered if his bountiful spirit would survive. Yet thanks to his church activities, he was rarely alone during the day. Even though I was young, I noted how the people of our congregation flocked around him. They didn't just remember to check on him for the next week or two after the funeral, they kept checking on him month after month. One of those who was often there for him was the kindly Miss Stodgill.

Miss Stodgill was as active in church as anyone in my own family. And the fact that my parents served on almost every board, attended every service, taught Sunday school, and were a vital part of the song service, meant that this woman had to be totally immersed in the daily goings-on of the Munson church just to keep up with the Paynes. It seemed that we couldn't have had church without her. Her smiling face was as much a part of the building as the pews or the Stamps-Baxter hymnals.

As the months since Grandma's death passed and the church worked its way through vacation Bible schools, prayer meetings, special song services, and revivals, a few members may have noted that my grandfather and Miss Stodgill seemed to be growing closer together. Yet I don't think Grandpa and Miss Stodgill even recognized it at first; it was just something that happened. One day they were friends, the next they discovered a bond that made them more than that, and that bond led to marriage. A year after he had lost the love of his life, my grandfather was blessed with another.

When Grandma died, I never thought Grandpa would get married again. At that time I couldn't picture him with any other woman but my grandmother. Yet as I began to see the way Miss Stodgill made him laugh and smile, and as I watched the sparkle return to his eyes and the spring to his step, I knew that God had sent another to fill the void in our family's life. What I didn't realize was just what she would come to mean to me.

As my grandfather's world changed, my day-to-day existence remained pretty much the same. I still worked in the fields, went to school, looked after my little brother and sister, and sang at church and with our friends whenever I got the chance. Among all the routine days, one stood out.

Our church decided to purchase new hymnals, and a recently completed shaped-note hymnal published by the Stamps-Baxter Music Company in Oak Cliff, Texas, was the one we had to have. Dad volunteered to pick up the new books. It was more than an hour from Munson to Oak Cliff, so my father called the company to make an appointment. V. O. Stamps himself agreed to meet Dad at the publishing plant early one Saturday morning, and I begged to tag along.

Anytime a country boy got to go to the big city, it was a special day. A trip to Dallas, though only thirty miles from my home, was as rare as a winter snow in north-central Texas. That morning as we drove down the highway in our old truck, my eyes took in everything. I spotted new-model autos, gaped at fancy, brick homes, and marveled at all the places city people had to shop. Best of all, I was about to visit the center of the universe—the Stamps-Baxter Music Company.

At that time, Stamps-Baxter was the largest publisher of nondenominational hymnals in the world, touching millions each week. Hundreds of songwriters, including Alfred E. Brumley, Thomas Dorsey, E. M. Bartlett, and Ernest Rippetoe, supplied this group with some of the world's best new gospel compositions.

When we arrived at the plant that Saturday morning, V. O. Stamps was there as promised. His smiling face and booming voice greeted us as we walked in the door. Grabbing my father's hand, he shook it vigorously, then turned his attention to me. His grin assured me that I was welcome, and his firm handshake indicated that he thought of me as more man than a twelve-year-old boy. As for me, now face-to-face with my hero, I stood in awe.

In retrospect I probably should have quizzed V. O. about a thousand different things. After all, I had stockpiled at least a million questions about quartets, singing schools, and radio over the years. But times were different then. Little boys didn't tug on grown-ups' sleeves and ask anything that entered their heads. Children spoke only when spoken to. I not only knew the rule, but lived by it. Therefore, I just watched as my father and the singer/composer/publisher completed their business transaction. Before I knew it, and long before I was ready, we were on our way back to Munson with a truckload of hymnals and all my questions about the music business still unanswered.

As I unloaded the boxes at our church that day, I had no reason to believe I would ever see Mr. Stamps or visit his business again. With 20/20 hindsight, I realize my connection with Stamps-Baxter and gospel music never would have grown beyond unloading shaped-note hymnals and singing the songs written in them if it hadn't been for my grandfather's new bride.

When Miss Stodgill married my grandfather, she fully stepped into her role as a grandmother too. To the best of her ability, she not only spoiled us kids, but took an active interest in every facet of our lives. She wanted to know our interests and get a feel for our talents, and she never failed to encourage us to dream. She believed in big dreams as much as she believed in Christ. In her mind the two just seemed to work together.

My step-grandmother had long felt that I had musical talent, that my voice was a gift from God, and she thought my dreams of some-day singing on radio with a quartet were within reach. While the rest of my family members were wringing their hands in frustration over not having the money to provide me with training, this dear woman went into action.

In her simple print dress and homemade apron, she may have looked like everyone's next-door neighbor, but in truth she was a woman who turned "can'ts" into "cans." Her strong faith played an important part in this facet of her personality. She knew all about making mustard seeds grow.

In the spring of 1939, Grandma took her seat at the kitchen table and composed a letter. Using a pen and a plain sheet of paper, she wrote the simple story of my life. That was her way of introducing me to V. O. Stamps. She explained how I listened each day to the Stamps' broadcasts, how the high moment in my life had been attending their concert in Josephine, how everyone in church thought I had the best voice they had ever heard, and then she added that it was her desire to help me fulfill my dream of one day getting to sing with a gospel quartet like the Stamps.

In closing, Grandma informed Mr. Stamps that if she had any money at all, she would gladly give it up to send me to his singing school. Yet, as all the Paynes were just poor dirt farmers who had to work odd jobs just to make enough money to keep food on the table, there was no way that she or anyone else in the family could afford to send her grandson to school. Then she explained that it was break-ing her heart that our being poor was costing a twelve-year-old boy a chance at using his God-given talent.

I am sure my new grandmother must have prayed over that let-ter for some time before she sent it. I am just as sure she went to sleep that night feeling that her simple prayer-driven letter was going to move a businessman's heart. I even feel confident that she knew what was in the letter from the Stamps-Baxter Company she received in return a few weeks later.

V. O. Stamps himself had written to my grandmother to tell her not to worry about the cost of sending her grandson to singing school. He had been so moved by her love for her grandson that he personally was going to see that a place was reserved for him in the June Oak Cliff session. All that young Glen Payne had to do was show up; it wouldn't cost anything.

Mr. Stamps must have received hard-luck letters every day. Why did he respond so positively to my grandmother's simple words? I can't really say. Maybe he prayed and felt God leading him to reach out to Glen Payne. Whatever the reason, Mr. Stamps' invitation in 1939 shaped the rest of my life, for I had been given a rare opportunity to study and work with the best, to learn the fundamentals of music from the ground up.

In today's world where so many modern recording artists receive their musical training over four years in college, it is hard to conceive what a three-week summer music session meant to people like me. The Stamps Singing School was the Harvard of gospel music. Simple folks from churches big and small traveled across the country for a chance to study with some of the best-known musicians of the "shaped-note" world. I knew people who spent twenty years of their savings or who gave up lunch for a year to pay for the tuition. Some people even sold their most prized possessions. That is how much this school meant to those whose lives had been touched by the message and music of gospel. As I soon found out, most of us who attended that year were poor, proud, and saved!

The weeks leading up to the summer session seemed to drag by. It was like waiting for Christmas. I didn't brag to my friends about where I was going or dwell on it during family meals; nor did I stay up late talking to my brother and sister about the opportunity I was being given. During the Depression, talking about yourself was something people just didn't do. We certainly didn't brag about our blessings around people who hadn't experienced too many themselves.

The night before I was to leave for school, I suddenly began to experience doubts and fears. Oak Cliff, though only about forty miles away from my home, now seemed on the other end of the world. I had never been away from home and wondered if I could manage to live without my parents for three weeks. I also wondered if the people at the school would think I belonged. I even began to question whether Mr. Stamps would think his goodwill was wasted on one who was unworthy.

I hadn't been this scared since my first day at regular school, but I didn't show it as my dad drove me to the school. Even as the butterflies did loops in my stomach, I tried to act grown-up.

After I watched Dad drive off, I turned to take in the new world in which I had been placed. It was a lot different from my rural home environment. Cars, houses, and people were everywhere, and the Stamps-Baxter headquarters at Tyler and Jefferson Streets in Oak Cliff seemed the heart of it all.

The Bethel Temple, where I was to study for three weeks, seemed like a grand cathedral to me. I was used to tiny frame churches that held a hundred people. I didn't even know that such large churches existed outside of New York or Europe! Bethel could seat more than a thousand for each service, and it was air-conditioned too! The carpeting was so plush and pretty that I was surprised they let common people walk on it with their shoes on. I felt like a pauper in the King's court.

For a young boy whose singing had been limited to church and home, the Stamps-Baxter Singing School really was a new world. In a sense, it was like jumping from first grade to college in one day. My mind was in a whirl as I found myself going from ear training to music theory to harmony classes and to scores of other sessions that taught me more in my first two days than I had learned in a lifetime of singing up until that point. I should have been overwhelmed, but I wasn't.

Day after day I sang scales, read pages of shaped notes, and learned to harmonize and blend in a way that transformed the songs we were singing into more than mere words. The harmony now fully defined each song's message. By the third day, I had discovered that most of the other students, though much older than I was, were just as ignorant. Best of all, I discovered that my grandmother's faith had been well placed. I soaked up my lessons almost as quickly as my teachers poured them out. I was thrilled that I really could learn this stuff!

Because we couldn't afford a boardinghouse, I stayed with a family from Bethel Temple whom my parents knew. Staying in a modest home much like my own helped make my transition easier, and for this I was very grateful.

While the weekdays were filled with long hours of study and work, the weekends were a reward of singing and fun. The students and teachers piled into buses and traveled to singing conventions in communities around Dallas. There we not only heard great choirs and quartets, but we also got to perform new material in groups. Seven hundred students made for some powerful-sounding choruses. I had felt gospel music stir my soul many times in church, and even singing in the fields had brought me closer to God, but when we sang in these weekend settings, it was almost like experiencing the Rapture. A spirit and a joy I had never imagined engulfed me. The music lifted me to heights that I didn't know existed.

For three weeks I learned, grew, and gained confidence. By graduation, which consisted of all-night singing at the Sportatorium, I felt assured that my dream of becoming a gospel music singer was within my reach. Of course, a twelve-year-old's view of reality is usually a bit skewed. Even as I joined more than ten thousand others at that final singing, I really hadn't a clue as to how much time, effort, work, and sacrifice it was going to take to realize my ultimate dream of being a part of a radio quartet.

Somewhere in the audience at that all-night singing was a woman who did know that I had a lot more to learn. Yet at that moment she wasn't worrying about the future; she just had pride in her eyes and assurance in her heart that things were going as they should. Without the faith and love of my step-grandmother, my dream never would have become more than a child's fantasy. Her letter opened the door to a world of opportunities and a life of doing what I loved. With faith, prayer, and love she paved my way!

{ chapter eleven }

FINDING AND
LOSING A PLACE

THE SPIRITUAL HIGH of the Stamps-Baxter school was soon replaced by long summer days in the cotton fields. During the thirties, a farm boy of thirteen was treated like a man, which meant working from dawn until supper, often at backbreaking tasks under an unforgiving Texas sun. I returned to the fields just in time to feel the full wrath of hot, humid July days. Yet even the heat of the summer days didn't quell my voice. With sweat pouring through my clothes, I would still be singing gospel songs as I worked from row to row.

The old Stamps radio shows might have given birth to my love of gospel music, but it was the school that baptized me in it. Beginning in the summer of 1939, I woke up thinking about harmony and drifted off to sleep dreaming about performing with my own group on the radio. However, I still hung on to a few childhood interests too.

Beyond toiling in the fields and singing quartet harmonies, my life was probably not unlike many young Texans my age. When rain kept me out of the cotton patch, I spent my days listening to *The Lone Ranger*, *The Shadow*, *Amos and Andy*, and the play-by-play of my two favorite baseball teams, the St. Louis Cardinals and the Texas League's Dallas Rebels.

Even though I loved the Cards and Rebs and knew the players' names and statistics, and even though I played a pretty good first base, a new glove or bat wasn't as important as getting hold of the latest songbook from Stamps-Baxter. Many of my friends thought I was crazy in this respect! They just couldn't identify with my dreams.

Thanks to my parents and a family who lived down the road, I was able to build a little of my dream each week. My dad, Everett and Vernon Vance, and I formed a gospel group known locally as the Munson Quartet. With Mom playing the piano, we sang at singing conventions in small towns like Terrell, Wills Point, and Royse City. At churches and under tents, my voice supplied the second tenor or alto parts. Songs such as "Give the World a Smile" and "Telling the World About His Love" enabled us to share good news of faith with hundreds each month. Rarely a weekend went by without our raising our voices heavenward.

During the week, we spent hours working out harmonies in our little living room. When I wasn't harmonizing, I was quiet, almost withdrawn, and spent a good deal of time alone. I just didn't have much self-confidence. It is a wonder I ever found the courage to sing in front of anyone. How I developed into a gospel music performer is a testimony to the people the Lord placed in my life, especially my parents, who were behind me every step of the way! Without two generations of love and encouragement, I doubt my voice ever would have reached beyond the lonely cotton fields.

In addition to my mother's parents, Grandpa and Grandmother Payne gave me a sense of what it meant to be a Christian in every facet of my life. They weren't singers and they didn't attend singing conventions, but they were the most devoted Christians I had ever known. Their faith enabled them to believe they could accomplish anything as long as God was with them.

The Paynes lived in Rockwall, Texas, and I was sure they were the glue that held the Rockwall Methodist Church together. Grandpa was a successful and respected businessman, and I loved to walk alongside him and listen to the townspeople greet him. He was always dressed in a white shirt and tie, even when he pumped gas or mowed his yard.

I wanted so much to be like my grandfather, and I doubt I could have picked a better role model. Ready to give the shirt off his back, he extended credit, gave loans, and helped people whom the banks wouldn't even acknowledge. He decided things in life based on faith, and I couldn't help but notice that his decisions usually worked out too. He taught me early that taking leaps was the only way to find one's limits, reach one's potential, and know true joy. Later, when it came time for me to take a few leaps on my own, I had his example to give me the confidence to go where I felt the Lord leading me.

My grandmother was more than just my grandfather's wife; she was his partner. She assisted him with his businesses, supported his decisions, and prayed for him when he took large steps of faith. I remember so well entering her kitchen in the middle of the morning, where she would be reading the Bible and praying. I was sure she knew more about God than any preacher I had ever heard.

Grandpa and Grandma Payne always made a huge deal out of Christmas. The entire family would gather at their house in Rockwall, where each grandchild would receive a special present. Complete with a decorated tree and homemade candy, their home was the essence of the holiday season. I was sure that even Santa didn't eat as well as we did on Christmas Day. In the midst of the Depression, Grandpa and Grandma Payne made me feel I had something special. They also made me believe I *was* something special.

I soon learned that being special and having special talents meant nothing if one wasn't willing to work. My father and two grandfathers had earned the respect of people in their churches and communities because they put legs to their prayers. Thus, I never felt I was being mistreated by working on the farm. Instead, I wanted to pull my own weight. This desire would stand me in good stead in the future as I pursued a career in the world of music. But at that time it just served to make me a bit happier than my friends who couldn't figure out why their fathers expected so much from them.

A lot of my buddies thought I was crazy because I worked so hard. When I wasn't working in our fields, I hired out to work for others. I chopped or picked cotton for a dollar a day for anyone who would have me. I also cleaned out barns, fed cattle, hauled hay, chopped wood, and did just about any job that no one else wanted to do.

A lot of people wondered why that Payne boy was so caught up in making money. They never saw me spending it, and they didn't know of any hobbies I had. They wondered why I was working so hard if I wasn't going to enjoy what I made. What they didn't know was that I deposited every penny into my singing-school account. Even though V. O. Stamps had already assured me a scholarship for my second year of schooling, I needed nice clothes for the term. So while other kids may have been wasting their money on gum, candy, and baseball cards, I was saving mine for something I thought far more special.

One spring day I came home from school intent on grabbing a bite to eat before I headed out to the fields. Before the door closed behind me, Mom grabbed me.

"Slow down," she demanded as I tossed my books on the couch and headed for the kitchen.

Smiling, I inquired what she needed.

"Glen," she began, a huge smile covering her face, "your two aunts in California wrote to us today. They are thrilled that you are using your voice to sing gospel music. Even though they are too far away to hear you sing, they wanted you to know that they are behind you all the way. They even sent five dollars as a gift for your fund!"

I couldn't believe it. No one had ever given me that much money! Five dollars sounded like a million bucks. I would have had to work a full week to make that much. With that sum of money I could buy a couple of shirts and have enough left over for socks! And they were sending it to me just because I was trying to learn about gospel music. Who would have thought that doing something I liked would have been worth that much money!

That five-dollar gift woke up my thirteen-year-old mind to the fact that singing gospel was something that could mean a great deal to others as well as to myself. I began to understand that the message behind the music was extremely important to a lot of people. It dawned on me that singing gospel music entailed a responsibility that didn't accompany country, folk, or pop. If I was going to sing gospel, I had to behave better than everyone else because a lot of people would be looking up to me.

To tell the truth, it was easy for me to be good when I had wonderful Christians all around me. I knew that straying from the straight and narrow involved nasty consequences; and wanting to please my parents, I was scared to death of disappointing them by tarnishing my father's and grandfather's good name. Even though I was young, my parents trusted me. This trust was something I wanted to hold on to. Even now, though all of them passed away long ago, I still feel it is important to live up to the standards they set.

Having matured another year and wearing new clothes, I returned to Stamps-Baxter in 1940. This time it was easier. I didn't get too homesick, I wasn't nearly as overwhelmed, and I had a lot more fun. By the end of that second term, I knew more music than most of the adults in our church. I also left school that year with the most incredible experience I had ever known ringing loudly in my heart and mind.

At the closing of the final all-night singing, the great songwriter Albert E. Brumley walked out to direct the choir in one of his most cherished compositions. You could have heard a pin drop as he lifted his hands and directed the first few notes of "I'll Meet You in the Morning." With the sun just peeking over the city and the first rays of light creeping into the auditorium, I was awed by the richest, fullest, and most profound presentation of a musical prayer I had ever heard. Chills ran up and down my spine, and I fully expected the Lord himself to return at the very moment the voices finished this hymn of praise. What a way to end a term and to celebrate the Savior whose music had brought me to the school in the first place!

This music had allowed me to *feel* heaven, a feeling I never wanted to give up. I vowed that I wasn't going to quit trying to become part of a group that could bring this kind of emotion and spirit to others. My family also had known for some time that I was driven to perform gospel music. After I returned from the 1940 school, they must have sensed that I was committed to this goal above all others.

Throughout the next year, I repeated the cycle I had started the year before. I worked, earned money, tried to improve my singing, and prepared for another term of school. I couldn't wait to go back and find my place in the world of gospel music. Yet in the midst of my preparation, in the midst of my year-long high, my world suddenly came crashing down when over the radio I heard the news that my mentor had died.

V. O. Stamps' sudden death crushed me. It was like losing a member of my family. I mourned for days, missing his voice on the radio and wondering what singing school would be like without his big hand patting me on the back from time to time. As my thoughts turned to school, I began to realize that without V. O. I might not even get to attend the Stamps-Baxter Singing School, for he had offered me the scholarships in 1939 and 1940. Would anyone else care enough to make sure that I got a scholarship in 1941? And if I couldn't go, how was I going to continue pursuing this dream that had become my passion?

I was so worried about losing my spot at the next term that even my parents sensed this concern was wearing on me. They contacted V. O.'s brother Frank, who quickly dropped me a line informing me that the school wouldn't be complete without my presence and that my scholarship would stand for as long as I needed it. Never had words so soothed my soul. And though I missed V. O., his brother soon took his place as the man who directed my own dreams as well as the school itself.

For the next two years, my three weeks at the summer school meant more to me than the other forty-nine weeks of the year. The masters of gospel music worked with me on ear training, sight training, harmonizing, and music theory. I was learning from Ernest Rippetoe, W. W. Combs, C. C. Stafford, and even Frank Stamps. These men shaped my life more than anyone outside my own family ever would. I wanted to be like them and sing, write, and teach like them. I wanted to earn the respect that they had earned and walk with the Lord the way they walked.

In my final year of schooling, the people at Stamps-Baxter put me together with a young piano player named Hovie Lister. He was incredible! Anyone who listened to him play swore he found new notes between the keys. I don't know how he did what he did, but I sure was pleased to be singing with him. Joining us in the Stamps-Baxter Quartet were Harold Davis, Cecil Roper, and Neely Ham.

Though still in high school, I suddenly found myself on bills with many of the regular Stamps quartets. And though World War II had severely curtailed travel, we continued to work conventions in places like Greenville, Texas, and singings all around Dallas. Frank asked me to contact him when I finished high school. He wanted to offer me a job with the organization. I could hardly believe it! I held my dream in my hand and couldn't imagine anything stopping me now!

No sooner had I learned that Frank Stamps appreciated my talent, than I was greeted by an event that shook my faith. The blow that crushed me involved a very natural process—my voice was changing. From being good enough to sing on a 50,000-watt clear-channel radio station for millions, suddenly I wasn't even good enough to sing with the Munson Quartet. On top of that came another blow.

Just as my voice gave out, my dad got a job in Dallas. Suddenly the country boy was moving to town, and I simply didn't have the confidence to take advantage of the change. Rather than go back for my senior year of school, I just quit. The schools in the city were too big and too intimidating for me. Unable to sing, living in unfamiliar surroundings, I was completely lost. I picked up a few dollars working odd jobs before I finally landed at one of the town's best bakeries.

With time on my hands, a war at the door, and no ability to sing, I was miserable. Without music, I suddenly had no dreams. Though everyone told me my voice would return in time, I simply didn't believe them. As far as I knew at that moment, my dreams and my life were over. I was going to be an untalented nobody forever. What use would the Lord have for me now?

chapter twelve

THE CHRISTIAN SOLDIER

Feeling adrift, I performed a series of odd jobs until I finally had a chance to make some real money. I landed a job at Mrs. Baird's, the largest bread company in Texas. I worked at Mrs. Baird's bread store until that job played out, then I found a job at a dry cleaners. Whether it was working with bread or old suits, I felt as if I were sleepwalking through life, using my back and my brain but not putting my heart into it. I worked hard and was a solid employee, but ultimately the jobs meant nothing to me.

When my family moved back to Rockwall, I stayed on in a rooming house in Dallas. As I moved from job to job, my treks across south Dallas would sometimes take me by the Stamps-Baxter Music Company. I would stand across the street and gaze longingly at the building, but I never went in. Stamps-Baxter had been the center of my universe, but no more. Now the world was focused on Japan and Germany. Even people who sat in the pews at the tiny churches in Munson and Josephine thought of little else. Everyone was talking about the war, and it seemed that everyone had a loved one in the middle of this life-and-death struggle.

Like most people, I was trying to keep up with the war too. I had friends on the front line. In 1944 I began to seriously consider whether a uniform could give me a fresh start! But before I could enlist or Uncle Sam could call me, Frank Stamps tracked me down. He wanted me to try out for one of his quartets. I was shocked! I hadn't sung in more than a year, and the last time Frank had heard me I had sounded terrible. I had all but given up on the idea of working for Frank again. Nevertheless, his interest gave me a bit of hope.

Frank didn't know where I lived and probably wouldn't have been able to find me had it not been for Harley Lester. One day I had stopped by a local radio station to listen to his quartet and visit. As we talked, Harley encouraged me to give the Stamps a try, but I told him I just didn't have the voice to make things work. Harley knew I was too shy to pick up a phone and ask for an audition, so he talked to Frank about me. Once again the Lord was looking out for me.

When Frank and I met, he explained that a lot of the singers had enlisted or had been drafted into the army. At the moment when people needed entertainment and inspiration, it was hard to find performers. He had been beating the bushes looking for talent when Harley had mentioned seeing me.

Frank figured my voice would have settled by now and that I could handle the tenor parts again. When he heard me sing that morning, I was surprised he didn't change his mind. My voice had settled, but it was a bit lower than before. I had been so nervous and rusty during the audition, I thought I had ruined my chances. Yet as God would have it, Frank was looking for a second tenor part, and somehow he thought he had heard a solid second tenor voice during the audition. When he told me I had the job, I was in shock! For the first time in more than a year, I was truly happy. I was feeling so good that I wanted to hug everyone I met.

The Stamps-Baxter organization paid me twenty-five dollars a week. I gladly would have worked for nothing, but I didn't tell them that. Each weekday morning at 6:30 I sang on KRLD with the Stamps-Baxter Quartet. What a thrill it was to know that my family was listening each day. The rest of the workday found me in the publishing plant making songbooks. It was hot, hard work, but it beat making bread or cleaning clothes. I loved every moment of it!

Because of the war and gas rationing, our quartet didn't travel much. Our longest trip was to Hot Springs for the Arkansas State Singing Convention. We primarily sang at local churches and small Dallas-area venues. From time to time, we also teamed up with groups such as the Chuck Wagon Gang for a large show.

Though I was a part of the company's leading quartet, I soon found out that my main job was sales. The goal of our live performances was to sell the latest edition of the Stamps-Baxter songbooks.

So while we performed all of the old favorites like "Kneel at the Cross," "Did You Ever Go Sailing?" "Jesus Hold My Hand," and "I'll Fly Away," we also sang the songs from our latest catalog. By pushing new songs from books such as *Favorite Songs and Hymns, Radio Favorites*, and *Select Radio Songs*, we were selling songbooks and doing good things for the company's bottom line. We all understood that our five dollars a day came from songbook sales, not ticket sales. So pushing the books was important! As shy as I was, I convinced people that hymnals were a good buy.

Those days in 1944 spent with the Stamps-Baxter Quartet were the best times I ever had known. Most of the men who worked with me were my father's age or older, and they treated me like a son. Each freely passed along to me the craft he had helped make so popular throughout the South, and each gave me self-confidence. From them I learned to perform in a professional manner. Nothing got past them—not the way I wore my one suit or how I spoke to the fans who caught up with us after our shows. I was being groomed by Frank and my mentors to be a gentleman. As the weeks turned into months, this grooming led to my feeling mature and confident for the first time.

As my self-confidence grew, I found that singing for a live audience became more meaningful. At first I had been afraid to study the faces of those who came to hear us. But as I became more comfortable, I began to note the smiles and tears our music created. As I studied my audience, I began to realize that I could feel real joy and emotions being channeled back to me through them. They were reflecting the message of our songs on their faces, and I loved what I was seeing and feeling. It made me realize that I was doing something important, making a real difference in people's lives. In the middle of a war, many people were looking for a way to strengthen their faith and ease their doubts, and our music seemed to create a path for them to do both of these things. As time went on, I couldn't imagine anything I could do in life that would be more important to God than what I was doing. I had found my calling.

Each day before we went on the air at KRLD, I would listen to the announcers reading the reports of the previous day's battles. Places I had never heard of now became as familiar to me as Munson,

Josephine, and Dallas. Normandy, Guam, Wake Island, and a hundred other names were burned into my mind each day. The thoughts of war so surrounded me that often at night, even as a gospel song danced in my head, I wondered what it would be like to be landing on a beach and shooting at another human being.

It was ironic that I was singing about the joy of heaven while so many kids my age were fighting and dying in a man-made hell. Yet sing I did, and pray I did. Though I loved my country and was proud to be an American, a part of me wanted the war to end before I had to discover whether I had the courage to land on that beach and draw a bead on another man. At the time, I thought I was the only one who selfishly prayed for peace. Little did I guess that millions of others felt the same way.

I was certain my prayers for peace had been ignored when, just after the new year in 1945, I got my draft notice. As soon as I showed it to Frank, he told me that he had the pull to get my service deferred. Though I was scared to death, I wouldn't let him use his contacts. I knew I had a duty to perform.

The day after Valentine's Day I spent the night with Frank and Sally Stamps. We talked about my early days at the singing school, about my growth as a singer, and about all the opportunities that would be awaiting me when I got back home. We continued to talk until late into the night, but what we didn't mention were my fears, my thoughts of death and dying, and my doubts about my courage. As those thoughts kept me awake that night, I am sure they haunted Frank too.

The next morning Frank had deep, dark circles under his eyes. On the air he announced that he was proud that one of the Stamps' own was on his way to serve his country. He dedicated a song to me and urged the audience to pray on my behalf. As I sang my last few numbers, I wanted to look Frank in the eye and let him know just how much I appreciated his support. Yet each time I caught his eye he turned away.

After our fifteen minutes of air time were up, I walked outside into the crisp February morning with Frank and Sally. It was a glorious, sunny day, but in my mind it was cloudy and gloomy. Just down the street was the induction center where I would begin my new life.

Picking up my bag and turning to say good-bye, I saw huge tears streaming down Frank's cheeks. Hugging my neck and patting me on the back, he struggled to say good-bye.

Not wanting to show Frank how scared I was or how much I dreaded going, I quickly turned around and walked down the sidewalk away from him. I was several yards away before I glanced back over my shoulder and saw him waving. Nodding my head, I bit my bottom lip and resolutely moved forward toward my destination.

The next few days passed in a blur. I barely remember standing with a group of other scared boys and taking my oath. I rode a bus from Dallas to San Antonio, then went on to basic training at Fort Hood, Texas. Soon I was working as hard as I had in the cotton fields back home.

From dawn to dusk, we trained—shooting, marching, climbing, running, peeling potatoes, and shining shoes. For the first time in my life, I was without a spare moment to listen to the radio or thumb through a songbook. My life revolved around the daily letters from home and from Harley Lester. I read them again and again each night before I climbed into my bunk. Even as fatigue tore at my aching body and darkness descended, I continually wondered whether I could shoot another human being.

I signed up for IRTC because I thought it meant I would become a radio man. Little did I know that I had joined the infantry. From Fort Hood I was shipped to San Antonio. There we drilled for duty in Europe. But in the midst of my training, Germany surrendered. Suddenly everyone's eyes shifted to the other side of the world. We would invade Japan.

We all knew what that meant. The Japanese had earned a reputation of fighting to the last man. Any attempt to take their homeland would be met by the kind of resistance none of us had ever imagined. As I looked around at the boys surrounding me, I knew that a lot of us would never make it back home. I wondered which ones would be fortunate.

In the midst of my personal battle with fear that went with the unknown, a letter from Harley caused me to doubt even the very thing that gave me a sense of identity and security. Frank Stamps had walked away from the Stamps-Baxter organization. In a battle over the importance of the quartets as opposed to the songbooks, Frank had decided to start his own company. His Stamps Music group would print songbooks, but he would push the quartet part of the business even more than had been done in the past. I had always assumed that if I survived the war, I would have a job at Stamps-Baxter. Now, with the split, I wondered whether there would be a place for me at either organization. Because of my close friendship with Frank, the old company probably wouldn't want me. Yet I wondered whether Frank's company would be able to support me and all the other quartet singers.

My anxieties were quickly displaced by larger fears as I was shipped from San Antonio to Paris, Texas, and then on to Oregon. Our group received our chilling orders to prepare for the Japanese invasion. As our ship moved across the Pacific, I read old letters and thought of home. Overcome by a feeling of fear and doom, I kept to myself and talked little.

Around me were hundreds of young soldiers. A few were relishing the thought of landing on the enemy's own turf. Some were even bragging about what they would do to the Japanese once we landed. But most seemed pensive like me, sitting quietly, wrapped in private thoughts.

We were a day out of Pearl Harbor when the announcement came. The ship's intercom broadcast the news that America had dropped an atomic bomb on Japan. At that moment, none of us realized just how powerful this new weapon was. I prayed that it would bring the Japanese government to its knees, but I doubted that it would.

At Pearl Harbor we heard the news of the second bombing, and then came word of the surrender. A part of me wanted to jump for joy like everyone else. Yet even in a sea of joyous soldiers, I felt strangely alone. I was thrilled that I wasn't going into combat, but I wondered what would happen next. Where would the army send us now?

Even as all of Pearl Harbor reveled in victory celebrations, we boarded an eastbound troop ship. We would not land until we had docked in Manila and had become a part of the occupation army. I would be stationed in the Philippines for over a year, most of my time spent with the 86th Blackhawk Division. We trained as though we would be deployed into another war area the next day—mock battles, shooting drills, combat readiness courses, and days spent out in the jungle. Rumors of all kinds of wild things spread, even of attacking the Soviets. Yet none of the swirling rumors grew into fact, and over time, I was moved from play battles to driving a truck that hauled troops who were on their way home.

Even though the war was over, we were reminded that we still had enemies and that some of them were killing our men. Because of the remoteness of the Japanese forces in the Philippines, many of their troops never got word that a peace treaty had been signed. These soldiers were still shooting at anyone wearing an American uniform. Though I was rarely put in danger, I didn't feel safe until I was pulled from training and truck driving and transferred to the PX.

My last two months overseas were spent much like a civilian. I got up, worked my shift, then returned to my room. For the first time in a year and a half, I had time to think about home, write letters, and plan for the future.

The mail I received from home filled me in on the farm and caught me up on the Stampses. In both cases, most of the news I received was good. My family was doing well, prosperity had returned to the area, and my little brother and sister were growing up strong, smart, and well behaved.

Harley Lester informed me that Frank Stamps had made a go of his new business. Not only were his quartets building larger and larger audiences in Texas and throughout the South, but his publishing business was doing well too. He had signed up some of the nation's best gospel songwriters and was carving into the market that had once been the sole province of Stamps-Baxter.

Still, I questioned if I was prepared to return to quartet work. I hadn't sung the entire time I had been in the service, hadn't joined a group, hadn't been part of a military choir, and hadn't even let on to my army buddies that I could sing. I was simply too shy to share my talents with the guys around me. When a few of them gathered around a piano or picked up a guitar and began to sing old favorites, I remained on the sidelines. My shyness was so painful that I wondered constantly whether I was good enough not only to sing but to attempt anything other than my normal duties. I may have been considered solid and mature beyond my years because I had never gotten into trouble by drifting from the moral standards of my youth, but I knew I still had a lot of growing up to do.

When I got my orders to report for transfer back to the States, I was deliriously happy. I couldn't wait to go home. A slow boat took me from the Far Pacific to California, and then I was shipped across country to Texas. After what seemed a lifetime of travel, I was finally set to be discharged in San Antonio in November 1946. Yet all the while the officers were filling out forms supposed to muster me out of the service, they were attempting to get me to reenlist. They sold me on everything from the quality of life the army would offer now that the war was over to the extensive training I could receive in a wide variety of technical fields while completing another hitch. I listened politely but never even considered reenlisting. While they spoke of the exotic places I could visit in the army, all I could think about was the loneliness of being away from home and the awful taste of powered eggs and milk.

Finally discharged, I flew to Dallas under the cover of night. Close to home at last, I hopped on a bus to Rockwall. It was one A.M. when I finally walked up to my parents' house. I stood in front of the porch for a few seconds taking in the sights and smells of home. Then, under a clear Texas sky, I paused and thanked God for bringing me safely home. With a lump in my throat and my heart pounding faster than the speed of light, I strolled onto the porch and knocked on the door. Waking from a deep sleep, my dad and mom were shocked to see me. After hugs and kisses and shouts of happiness, we all went into the kitchen, where Mom cooked me the best tasting fresh eggs I had ever eaten.

We didn't sleep much that night, nor did we get much work done the next day. When we weren't talking, we were either staring at one another or looking out over the peacefulness of fall in Texas. It felt so good to be home. My eyes, my heart, and my mind took it all in in short bursts. I sipped the emotions and feelings, savoring each. Even a familiar old chair brought up passions that I couldn't begin to describe. Just raking my hand across the dining room table or scooping up a handful of Texas dirt brought a smile.

For a day, I strolled through my magical, peaceful world, talking with old friends, swapping stories, sharing memories, and looking at old and new photographs. Nevertheless, I knew I wasn't quite home yet; I still had to make the trip to Oak Cliff to find out whether I had a spot in a gospel music quartet. This time I wasn't going to wait for Frank Stamps to call me and convince me to come back. I was finally ready to walk into his office on my own.

chapter thirteen

BLENDING IN
AFTER THE WAR

As WELCOME AS I HAD BEEN at my parents' home, I felt a new sense of welcome as I walked through the doors of the Stamps Music Company. As I excitedly searched for old friends in the new company, I knew that I couldn't go back to the Stamps-Baxter Music Company down the street. When thirteen employees had left to form a new company, a battle for trade had begun. Even before I shipped back to the States, I knew I would have to place my loyalty with one group or the other. There could be no running back and forth after I made my initial choice.

Even before Frank Stamps struck out to try it on his own, the Stamps family had paved the way for me to be in this business, and they had treated me as though I were family. They had paid for my schooling, given me my first real job, put me on the radio, and kept up with me when I was overseas. Now they were excited that I was back, and they offered me a job.

Loyalty is something my family taught me by example from the time I took my first steps. You stuck with friends and relatives through the good times and the bad. Your word bound you to those who looked out for you. And when someone gave you something, you spent the rest of your life trying to repay it. Deep down I knew I could never repay Frank and V. O. Stamps, but I was going to try as hard as I could anyway.

As I walked in on that first day, I felt like a long-lost son or brother returning home. Everyone was excited to see me, even those whom I had never met before. I shook scores of hands, received numerous hugs, got the grand tour of the humble new facility, and heard stories of how the business had changed. After all of the back-slapping and storytelling ended, I was informed that I quickly needed to find a place to live because I was to be part of a quartet within weeks.

I was overjoyed to hear those words. It was great to be needed and wanted so much. I also realized, however, that this organization was expecting a great deal out of me, which was more than a little scary. After all, it had been almost two years since I had sung a note.

To get my feet wet, I accompanied the Lester-Stamps Quartet on a concert trip just four days after getting out of the service. Though I was there only to observe, it felt good to be back in the world of live gospel music. The joy of hearing the old songs, the excitement of unveiling new material, and the thrill of seeing the crowds respond got me juiced up. In my heart I knew this was the reason I had returned home.

I discovered a rooming house in Oak Cliff, just a short walk from the Stamps' offices, and hit the ground running. Still technically a member of the United States armed forces—my official discharge was a few weeks away—I was now serving with a much smaller group, whose battles were fought with songs instead of guns. It was almost like being in drill camp too. Haskell Mitchell, a fine bass singer; Loy Hooker, one of the area's best tenors; and Harley Lester, our lead singer, pushed me to come up to speed in a hurry. They had to have a baritone, and they didn't have time for me to sing my way back into shape. Hence, with Lawrence Ivy playing the piano, I met daily with the guys for hours on end and learned all the songs, expanding my range and rediscovering the harmonies I had been missing so badly.

Even with all the work we were doing, I think it probably would have taken months to get into the shape that I felt I needed to be in to properly fill my spot with the other men. Nevertheless, I had less than two weeks before I was not only pushed out on the concert trail, but was singing each weekday on the early morning gospel show on KRLD radio.

In the past, moving this fast would have all but swamped me. But my military experience stood me in good stead. Pressure didn't affect me as it once had. While I wasn't swaggering with confident self-assurance, I wasn't a tepid unsure kid anymore, either. I had a growing degree of self-esteem, a recognition that I did have some God-given talents, and maybe most importantly, I felt the respect of those around me. While I knew I would be a better singer a few months down the road, I was confident that I wasn't going to make a fool of myself or let the group down.

It didn't take long to discover that the world of gospel music in 1946 was much different than it had been only two years earlier. Some of it had to do with the fact that I was with a new and energetic company that was determined to make its mark. Yet I doubted that that alone accounted for the way huge crowds were turning out wherever we appeared. I wasn't, however, a seasoned enough pro to know for certain what was driving this mighty thirst for gospel music.

Before, I had worked in quartets only during the early years of the war. Gas rationing had curtailed almost every group's concert tours. My duties then had been pretty simple—singing on the radio and working in the plant. Our few concerts had been modestly attended. But now the numbers were overwhelming.

Perhaps this surge was part of the joyous postwar atmosphere, perhaps it was because so many had prayed so hard and long for peace, or perhaps it was just because there was money in a lot of pockets. Whatever the case, we were selling tickets by the armfuls and playing in packed churches, schools, and auditoriums. It seemed like everyone from Future Farmers of America to the American Legion wanted us for fund-raisers. And wherever we went, no matter the venue, people wanted to meet us, ask questions, and tell us how much our music meant to them. They also wanted to take something special home as a reminder of our presentation.

To meet demands for products other than songbooks, we packed into a recording studio on January 1 to cut several gospel music sides. In those days recording wasn't very well planned, took hours rather than weeks to complete, and used no outside production or performing talent. Making a gospel record in 1946 was an unsophisticated process, not much different than doing a radio show. We would run over the designated songs a few times, find our parts, discuss anything we wanted to change in the arrangement, and then sing. There was no layering, few retakes, and none of us would have known what looping was if we had been asked to do it. We simply tried to concentrate and do the very best we could, and then we went home. That was all there was to it. What people heard on our old "78s" was very much what they heard on their radios, the very real and unenhanced sounds of the Lester-Stamps Quartet. Yet that didn't stop the records from selling by trunkloads.

Concerts were much simpler affairs too. For larger shows, we used a small, portable sound system consisting of one microphone and a little box of speakers no bigger than a standard suitcase. All of us would sing into the mike, and Lawrence would pound hard enough on the piano to be heard. Even though the sound was never more than adequate and the piano provided for us was usually horribly out of tune, it didn't seem to matter. The people still came, clapped, and called out for more.

We were hot, and Frank Stamps made the most of our popularity by pushing us hard. Each morning we were up and on our way to the radio show before the sun rose. After that, we would grab breakfast, work a few hours in the publishing house, and then pile into an old Buick or Ford. With one of us driving while the others slept, we drove as fast as we could to make a nightly booking. In many cases the venue was hundreds of miles from Dallas and our schedule so tight we didn't even have time to stop and eat. As we arrived, we would hurriedly unload, look over the facility, find out how bad the piano was, and then practice a bit. After the show, we would sell our product, talk to fans, and finally pile back into the car and head for home.

The hardest dates were those in Oklahoma, Louisiana, or Arkansas. We were so far from Oak Cliff that we often would arrive back just minutes before the radio show went on the air. Tired, stiff, and rarely in top voice, we would pull our act together in time to do our radio spot. After breakfast we would start all over again.

It was a hard life, and I spent more time sleeping in the seat of a car than in my own bed. Rarely did I have days off. On weekends, when we didn't have a radio show, we would do three-day swings through sections of the country too distant to play during the week.

It is little wonder that many of the guys burned out, but for some reason I loved the pace. No matter how tired I was or how hard I was pushed, I ate it up. Performing on the radio each day and singing in front of live crowds each night meant more to me than anything I was missing, and I was missing a lot. I had little time for church, movies, dating, or socializing. Rarely did I get to travel the thirty miles home to see my family. Yet even as I watched other guys leave for jobs that had better hours and pay, I couldn't understand why anyone would ever quit singing gospel music. No matter the price, I thought it was worth it.

That must have been how Harley Lester felt. He was middle-aged, had never married, and seemed to live to sing. That's probably why he liked me as much as he did. I was a man after his own heart; in a very real sense, both of us were like Catholic priests, married to a profession we viewed as a calling that allowed no time for anything else. The reward of the work—singing the greatest music ever written and having people tell you that your music raised their spirits and drew them closer to God—made the sacrifice worthwhile.

In 1947 we traveled to California. What a trip it was! We got to meet several groups who traveled in different areas than we did. As a result, we learned some new songs, heard some fabulous new arrangements, and got to know some great people who loved the business as much as Harley and I did.

One group I enjoyed a great deal were the Weatherfords. Earl and Lily Fern were special people. To them gospel music was a calling, not just a business. As taken as I was with them, I didn't think they even noticed me. I would later discover that Earl had made as many mental notes about me as I had about him. His notes would someday shape my life in a very special way.

In October 1948 I was transferred from the Lester-Stamps Quartet to the Stamps All-Star Quartet. Haskell Mitchell came too, and we joined singers Roger Clark and Clyde Garner with Jack Taylor at the piano. While the name of my "team" changed, my own life remained the same. My new quartet still sang on the early morning radio show, still hit the concert trail each night, and still worked at the plant whenever we had a few spare hours.

Twice a year everything stopped for three weeks of singing school. The period when I worked for the Stamps was the height of popularity for the singing school movement. We had as many as a thousand people signing up per session. Just down the block the Stamps-Baxter group was doing every bit as well. It seemed like everyone in the South had gone crazy for gospel music.

For the first few years I really looked forward to the schools. I didn't have any responsibilities at the sessions, so I would work in the plant for eight hours, go home at the end of the shift, and watch a movie or listen to the radio. By the late forties, Frank decided I should teach voice in the singing school. Though I wasn't going to tell my boss, I had no idea how to teach voice. And if Frank knew that, he didn't let on. Because of the overwhelming number of students who were attending the sessions, he had to draft anyone he could. Mustered into the faculty ranks, I was assigned a group of students and put to work.

I ran my students through the paces of every singing drill I could remember from my student days. I praised them, assured them they were progressing, and corrected them in ways that didn't reveal my own inexperience. Even though I felt inadequate, most of my students seemed thrilled with me. In their minds, I was the great baritone singer for the All-Star Quartet, and that made me an expert. What I said and taught was valuable information they couldn't get anywhere else.

Often at the all-night singings that signaled the end of our sessions, individual vocalists would perform in front of the thousands who had gathered to celebrate the evening of praise and worship. I was shocked when one of my students stepped to the middle of the huge stage to display her newly learned skills. Yet I felt what many new teachers feel as they watch one of their pupils—pride. Standing in the back, my eyes and ears glued to center stage, I grew apprehensive and confused when I noted that the young woman was alone. I knew that she didn't have the voice to pull off an a cappella solo, yet this appeared to be just what she was going to attempt. Then she floored me. In a move that would become legendary in singing school lore, instead of singing, my student began to whistle "Victory in Jesus." As one horrified teacher and an amused audience looked on, she whistled the entire song.

When the young woman finished, the crowd didn't know what to do. At the back of the room, I was looking for a place to hide. All around me were singing school teachers who couldn't wait to quiz me about the whistling method I had used on this young woman. In fact, they needled me for months. That solo haunted me for years and is still following me today. I am reminded of that young woman's performance every time I run into someone who knows me from the school.

While the whistling young woman may have made my life miserable for a few moments, I eventually came to identify with her. As I grew as a singer, I wanted to try my hand at doing some lead work. By 1950 I thought I was ready to get up in front of an audience and lead the group, but every time an opening for a lead singer came up in one of our quartets, Frank or Harley asked someone else to fill the position. They wouldn't let me fly on my own and wouldn't tell me why.

I guess there are times when even a satisfied person feels a need to have more. At the time, I thought maybe my ego was making me jealous of the others who always jumped ahead of me for the positions I wanted, but I now think it was the Lord's way of making me look at myself and take stock of what I wanted out of life. I was beginning to realize the obvious: I had allowed my life to become one-dimensional. Work was everything to me, more than it should have been. During these personal struggles, God may have been trying to get my attention, showing me that work alone could not make my life complete. But living and breathing each day at Stamps Music put me too close to the situation to realize this. What I didn't know was that I needed some space to grow, think, and live. Not all of the answers were going to come out of Oak Cliff, Texas. Still, blinded by drive and ambition, I stuck it out.

For two more years I was patient, waiting for my chance to sing lead in the organization. During that time, a young man named Ford Keith would come into my life and change my world forever.

I had known Ford since my first singing school days at Stamps-Baxter. He was my age, a wonderful singer, and an even better young man. His dream, like mine, had been to be the lead singer in a gospel quartet, but unlike me, he had made it. He had reached his goal with the Stamps-Ozark Quartet of Siloam Springs, Arkansas.

Though independent from Frank and his organization, the Stamps-Ozark Quartet still sold some of our music and sang some of our songs. That's how I knew they had starved out in Arkansas and then moved their business base to Wichita Falls, Texas. There on the flat, dry panhandle plain they had kept their original name and had carved out a solid reputation both on radio and at area concerts. With money in his pocket and doing what he had always wanted to do, it didn't seem that things could get much better for Ford. A small part of me couldn't help but wish for a life like his.

But just as Ford Keith was becoming a gospel music star, tragedy hit. He was struck with a severe form of kidney disease and was given just months to live. It was hard to hear about this young man dying; he had so much to live for. Finally, at the age of twenty-seven, both his voice and his heart stopped altogether.

I would later discover that Ford had pitched me to the other guys in the Ozarks. He thought I would make a great lead singer and wanted me to have that opportunity. When the group invited me to fill his spot, I was amazed. My prayers had been answered, only not in the manner or place for which I had prayed. As I packed my bags and said good-bye to the place where I had thought all my dreams were destined to come true, I wondered if I could succeed with a group that had suffered such a tragic loss. Could I give them what they needed? And just as importantly, would I be letting Frank down and being disloyal by leaving the Stamps Music Publishing Company? After years of knowing what every second of every day was going to be like before it happened, not knowing what was ahead was probably just what I needed.

) *chapter fourteen* (

TAKING THE LEAD

MY LIFE CHANGED more dramatically than I could have imagined. Suddenly I was living in a small Texas town rather than in a big city like Dallas. I was singing on regional rather than national radio, and the organization that now employed me was a lot more laid back than the folks in Oak Cliff had been. After what I had been doing, this was like taking a vacation with a nice bit of work thrown in.

My father's sister lived in Wichita Falls and insisted that I stay with her. I loved the dear woman, and having the chance to get to know her better appealed to me a great deal. Best of all, it would be like living at home and the rent would fit my meager budget.

Even before I unpacked my bags, I headed off to get to know my new partners. If I had apprehensions about fitting in, they vanished when I got into the same room with Pat Garner, Charles Barlett, Fred Bennett, and pianist Henry Slaughter. From that first meeting, I knew I had their complete trust. They didn't try to hide anything or hold anything back. They welcomed me with open arms, treated me as an equal, and showed me the ropes unique to their organization. Once we settled the business details, we moved on to music. Since they were singing most of the same songs I had already been performing with the Stamps All-Star Quartet, that went pretty smoothly as well. The only difference was that now I would be out front carrying the big load.

During our initial rehearsals, I sounded pretty good. I hit my notes, carried them well, and projected like a seasoned lead. But my first time in front of a radio mike, I felt myself tightening up. My knees turned to liquid, my throat went dry, and my stomach did flips. It seemed to me that I was rushing, yet if the others guys thought so, they didn't mention it. They just followed my lead. By the end of the show, with the Ozarks' solid backing, I was calmer, more assured, and felt that I really was the lead singer for the Stamps-Ozark Quartet.

KWFT was not a 50,000-watt clear-channel icon like KRLD. Our listening area was limited to the Texas panhandle, some of the plains, and a part of Oklahoma. And while there were more open spaces than big towns in this region, we didn't have any problem getting show dates. Every night some group wanted us to sing at their school, church, or lodge. Sometimes we even were booked to perform on a courthouse lawn or in an old cotton field. Wherever we went during those first few years, people by the hundreds would pile in old pickups and dusty sedans and make the trip to hear us.

In many ways, performing with the Stamps-Ozarks reminded me of the atmosphere of the first Stamps concert I had seen in Josephine, Texas. Just like the old Stamps group, we opened with a solid batch of gospel classics sung from a songbook published by the Stamps Music Company. We knew the songs by heart, but singing with the books helped us sell them at intermission and after the shows.

While I was used to singing from books and pitching the songs in the latest offering, nothing in my previous experience had exposed me to the style the Ozarks employed during the second half of the show. They called this segment the "Cigar Box Opry." Sandwiched in between the opening and closing group of gospel standards were country-style comedy and even some secular favorites. Our concerts seemed rooted not only in old church singings, but in classic medicine shows. Because we were the only professional performers many of our patrons had ever heard live, the guys in the Ozarks were convinced that we should offer a bit of everything. I wasn't wild about the Opry part of the show but came to realize it as something our audiences really appreciated.

Our shows were simple, direct, and honest; and the crowds seemed to reflect these same values. Many of them didn't have much but their pride, their faith, and the clothes on their back, but when we visited with them after the show, we realized that that was all they needed. They were happy and fulfilled. Having grown up in similar circumstances, I would have been shocked had it been any different.

I knew firsthand that hard times had been a way of life in rural Texas since well before the Depression. Even now with farm prices up, things hadn't changed all that much. People were living on the edge. One drought, one bad crop, an accident, or a death could wipe them out. The hard labor they had endured for years showed in their hands and weathered skin, but their eyes reflected something far different. Here one could see their spirit, love, and compassion. And it was the look in those eyes that made me proud, not just to sing for them, but to be considered one of them.

One of the best things about my new job was that I was making more money than when I had been a "spotlighted" star on KRLD in Dallas. And while I wasn't traveling across the country and singing on the West Coast occasionally, I still wasn't totally cut off from the excitement of big-time entertainment. W. B. Nowlin used us on some of his big bills in Dallas and throughout Texas. On rare occasions we would open for people like Eddy Arnold, the traveling Opry shows, and even a young up-and-comer from Memphis named Elvis Presley. At that time I didn't know what to make of him. I thought his performance was a little strange, yet I had to admit that he did have something unique that crowds loved. I didn't figure he would last long. I preferred the more laid-back approach of Eddy Arnold.

While we did well with live shows, our bread and butter was radio. The programs we did twice each weekday and once on Sunday morning set everything else up. We opened each weekday program with an early morning breakfast show sponsored by the Northern Star Cotton Seed Company. Nutrina Feeds paid our way at the noon hour as we served up a bit of gospel music to go with lunch.

We used a standard format on our two fifteen-minute weekday shows and on the Sunday morning half hour. On each we would sing a mix of old favorites, new songs, and special requests. We made sure that almost everything came from a Stamps Music Company book we were selling at that time. The listeners could send in a check or money order and receive a copy of the book. While they could sing our songs in their own homes, we could bill the Stamps Music Company for a sales commission. Between these commissions, our salaries from our two sponsors, and the fee the radio station gave us, our daily on-air work provided us a solid income as well as a great base from which to secure future concert bookings.

Compared to the workload I had been pulling in Dallas, I thought things were really easy in Wichita Falls. Just a couple of years after I joined the Ozarks, things got even easier. Through the use of the newly invented tape format, we were able to prerecord shows. While we still did the noon show live, we taped the early morning weekday show and the Sunday morning show, thus enabling us to schedule live performances further from home. It also gave me a chance to sleep in for the first time in my life.

At first I didn't know what to do with all the extra time. In the mornings, before we began to tape the early programs, I listened to the radio, read the paper, did some shopping, or even took a nap after our program. After the live show at noon, I had a few more hours to kill until we traveled to our evening date. While I didn't miss the long night trips, all-night traveling, or assembling songbooks, I quickly became bored. I just wasn't good at doing nothing.

Fishing was too dull. I didn't like waiting for a fish to bite my line. I wasn't much of a hunter either and had yet to find a young woman who seemed to be as perfect as I thought she should be. I might have gone crazy if I hadn't developed a passion for golf. Ironically, now that I had matured enough as a man to take on the responsibilities of a lead singer and a group leader, I was also discovering the joy of being a child.

Play time had never been a big part of my life as a kid. My youth had been spent helping my family and making my dreams come true. Now I was able to spend time on the links whenever I had the chance. I would play in the heat, cold, rain, and even when it was threatening snow. I loved hitting the ball and chasing it around the fairways. I loved even more the feeling of watching it go into the cup. Golf was a game where I could mark my scores, register my daily rounds, and document my progress as a player. I thrived on being able to see my game develop through my daily scores, and I also enjoyed working at and improving my skills. Up until this time I had no idea that any game could be so challenging and so much fun.

After a few months of "playing," I found I was more relaxed than I ever had been before. I was laughing more, getting to know people in ways other than just work, and noticing all the wonders of the world. For the first time in more than a decade I was hearing birds sing, watching flowers bloom, and getting a kick out of observing children playing in their yards. It was as if a whole new world had been revealed to me, a world I had been too busy to notice.

Looking back, I now believe God may have been testing me in Dallas. There things were intense; although I was working night and day and wasn't advancing in my profession like I wanted, I stuck with it. To me this proved that I really did have the desire to be a part of the music business. Once I had proven this to myself and those around me, I feel the Lord gave me Wichita Falls as a reward. Here I learned how to be not just a lead singer, but to enjoy God's world to its fullest.

Adding to the richness of my life during this period was the opportunity to become an active part of a church again. The Ozarks didn't work much on Sundays, so I eagerly joined my aunt at first as a visitor and then as a busy member of a local Methodist fellowship. I delighted in singing in the choir, participating in Sunday school classes, and even listening to the sermons. I had grown up in this environment, and now that I once again had the chance to be a part of it, I realized just how much spiritual benefit came through regular worship with a large group of people of all ages and backgrounds. I rediscovered that all people, even those who sang gospel music every day of the week, needed a steady dose of church life to keep them spiritually on track and growing.

While church and golfing became very important to me during this time, quartet music was still what drove me on a day-to-day basis. When we weren't working and I had a night off, I would travel for hours to hear another good gospel group. One night I convinced Charles Barlett to drive me down to Fort Worth to hear my old group, the All-Star Quartet.

It turned out to be a great night. I enjoyed seeing old friends, listening to them sing their songs, and walking around a familiar haunt. I was so excited that for most of the way home I filled Charles with stories of my old days in Dallas. It was well past midnight when our talk finally died down. With Charles at the wheel and the familiar signs along the road signaling we would soon be home, I should have been completely relaxed, yet for some reason I suddenly felt the hair stand up on the back of my neck. Shaking the sleep from my eyes, I spotted a cattle truck veering into our lane. Charles pulled the wheel hard to the right but not soon enough. We hit the truck head on, and our car was knocked across the road. For a few seconds the world stopped.

Miraculously, Charles and I had somehow escaped injury, but our car had been demolished. Had we been outsiders driving by, we would have thought that those in the car had been killed. Yet we had been delivered safe and sound. A few hours later, we were even able to sing on our radio show. I remember remarking, "Well, I guess the Lord still has something planned for us." Little did I realize then just how much more he had in store for me.

For five years things flowed as smoothly as a Lincoln V-12. Our radio shows continued to draw listeners, our sponsors continued to support us, and our concert calendar remained full. I was teaching Sunday school, playing several rounds of golf each week, and had even purchased my own car. I was almost thirty years old and feeling very positive about life in general. Then, without warning, the bottom dropped out, not once but twice.

A major drought hit the Panhandle in 1956. The rural economy got so bad that Northern Cotton Seeds and Nutrina cut back on advertising. Our radio shows were the first to be axed. Without the radio programs, our dates began to dry up too. By November things had become so bad that the other guys in the group wanted to quit. I tried to convince them to hang on for a few more months, but they had families to feed, so they walked away. Although I hated to see the Stamps-Ozarks Quartet die without a fight, I didn't blame the guys for giving up. None of us knew when good times would be returning.

Without the quartet, there was nothing left for me in Wichita Falls, so I packed my bags and drove back to my parents' house in Rockwall. I decided to rest up for a few weeks and then search for a new spot in a quartet after Christmas.

At first I enjoyed being home. I hadn't had a chance to visit with my family for a long time, and Mom's cooking sure beat the restaurant fare I had been eating. Yet after a few days of catching up, I was ready to get back to work. Frank Stamps called with a couple of offers, and I was tempted to take one of the open spots he had, but these jobs would have been a step backward. I didn't want to get into the grind of working night and day and catching a few hours of sleep in the backseats of big sedans. I had seen it make too many young men old. As the weeks dragged by, however, nothing better seemed to materialize.

I was practicing with a Methodist church choir for a Christmas program on December 20, 1956, when a family friend rushed in the side door of the church. He raced up to me, pulled me to one side, and broke the news that my father had been seriously injured in an automobile accident. At that moment the doctors didn't even know if he would live.

I will never forget that Christmas. The next few weeks I practically lived at the hospital. As my mother, brother, and sister waited for hopeful news, it became apparent that getting my dad back on his feet was going to be a lengthy ordeal. My mother believed that I had been forced out of gospel music so that I could be home to help the family through this difficult time.

As the days dragged by and we got the news that it would take months or even years before my father would be able to work, I too wondered if the reason I hadn't found a new job was because the Lord was pointing me toward home. Yet even as my mother tried to convince me to look for a job driving a truck or working in a factory, I couldn't help but believe that doing so would be throwing away years of experience and all the talent God had given me.

My life was awash with a million conflicting emotions. As I prayed for a miracle cure for my father, I had to question whether I desired this rapid healing for my sake or his. I didn't want to stay at home, yet this was what everyone believed I had to do. I wanted to tell my mother I had to get on with my own life, but I knew that I couldn't turn my back on my parents. Resolutely I finally told God that if this was what he wanted, then I would do it. His will was more important than everything else. From that point on, I turned my attention from gospel music to taking care of my mother and father.

{ chapter fifteen }

A NEW DIRECTION

By THE FIRST OF THE YEAR, we knew that my father would live, but we didn't know how much of his old life he would regain. The doctors told us that Dad would need several operations just to be able to walk. Always a strong and vigorous man, he was now bedridden, in constant pain, and completely dependent on others.

Not knowing what was ultimately in store for Dad was frustrating. I felt totally helpless. Though my mother was glad I was home, she got just as much moral support and comfort from her many friends who came by daily. At home and at the hospital, I seemed to be a fifth wheel.

Even though my father was facing the hardest battle of his life, he sensed my restlessness. He never really told me to get out of the hospital and pursue my dream, but everything he said seemed to point in that direction. And as much as I wanted to get back on the phone and search for a job with another quartet, the look in Mom's eyes anchored me to home. If God had another plan, he would need to help Mom understand.

About three weeks after the wreck, the phone rang. I had expected it to be a friend or relative inquiring about how my father was doing, but surprisingly the person on the line was aware of my father's plight and just wanted to talk with me about a job. I was shocked to be hearing from Earl Weatherford.

Without my realizing it, I had made a big impression on Earl when I had been with the Stamps organization in Dallas. Later Earl had listened to me on the radio performing with the Stamps-Ozarks. Around Christmas Earl had heard that the Stamps-Ozark Quartet had starved out. Three members of his own group, the Weatherfords, a pianist and two vocalists, had left to form a new quartet. Earl had to move quickly to fill these holes or lose his longtime spot with evangelist Rex Humbard's organization.

I knew the Weatherfords had been using a solid, young bass singer named George Younce. Though I had never met the man, I had heard enough to know that he was very good. I also knew that Danny Koker and Jim Hammel had been solid members of the quartet as well. But what I didn't know was that they had all taken off for Milwaukee. When Earl told me that he and his wife, Lily Fern, were all that was left of the group, I wondered if the Weatherfords weren't evaporating, much as the Stamps-Ozarks Quartet had just months before. Before I could tell him I had my hands full and couldn't even consider his offer, Earl assured me that things weren't that bad. He had found a new bass singer, Armond Morales, who had sung with the group before going into the service. Earl also believed that he could secure some pretty good dates once he added someone like me to the mix. In his mind, I was the linchpin.

I didn't know what to think. Earl wasn't offering a guaranteed income, and I was uncomfortable with the thought of singing in a mixed quartet. Nevertheless, I was impressed that he had gone to a great amount of trouble to track me down. I wondered if the Lord's hand wasn't in this offer. Rather than outright rejecting the offer like a logical man would have done, I decided to take time to pray and think about the offer.

The Weatherfords were based in Akron, Ohio, and that was a long way from Texas. Back then the Midwest was not a hotbed for gospel quartets, at least not like the South, but because of their affiliation with Rex Humbard, this group had something that few others could claim—solid support. Their link with one of the most popular young preachers in the nation was what convinced me that this was a chance worth taking. Yet I was still caught in a quandary: Should I leave home at this critical time?

A trip to the hospital assured me that I could do nothing for my father that wasn't being done already. What he needed was my love and support, and he knew he had that no matter where I was. After talking with him, I knew that he was not holding me back. Mom, however, was another story. Even though I was doing very little for her, she still seemed to think she needed me as a crutch. What would she think of me if I left? How would she handle it? I didn't ever remember being so troubled. After praying and feeling assured that God needed and wanted me to go to Ohio and sing again, I called Earl and informed him that I would be on my way as soon as I could get things in order at home.

As I expected, my mother was horrified when I broke the news. She felt betrayed and couldn't believe I would take a job nearly a thousand miles away rather than stay and help Dad get back on his feet. Though I assured her that I sensed the Lord's leading, she would have none of it. Through tears she begged me to reconsider. She thought it was time for me to settle down, get a job in the real world, marry some nice local girl, and start a family. When I told her I couldn't do that, she all but fell apart. It was as if I had stuck a knife in her back.

I had never done anything as hard as packing my bags and loading them into my old Plymouth. I felt I was breaking my mother's heart, the one thing I had sworn I would never do. For the first time in my thirty years of life, I believed that she was ashamed of me.

I drove through East Texas and then Arkansas with Mom's tear-filled face haunting me each mile. In Forest City, Arkansas, just as my will was about to break and I was about to turn around and head home, my car broke down. I was stuck hundreds of miles from home, halfway between a new world that called to me and an old one that wouldn't seem to let me go, and I wasn't sure what to do. Exhausted, emotionally spent, I fell against my steering wheel and begged God for help.

He answered my prayers even before I uttered them. When the old sedan broke down, I couldn't immediately turn around and rush back home. Even though I didn't want to, I had to wait to get it fixed. While I was waiting for my car to be repaired, I called home. Surprisingly, Mom had calmed down and seemed to accept the fact that I was doing what I felt I had to do. She was once again on my side and no longer ashamed of me. She was once again my biggest fan even if she didn't fully understand my reasons for leaving. Now, with her backing, I could continue on to Ohio and begin my new life.

When I arrived in Akron, I got a room, unpacked, and then met with Earl, Lily Fern, and Armond. Before we started rehearsing, I had an uneasy feeling about working in a group with a woman. To me a real quartet was made up of all men. I wasn't prejudiced; I just thought the blend didn't sound as good with a mixed group. But hearing Lily Fern sing was like an answered prayer. Her voice was beautiful, a breath of pure air on a spring day. The higher it rose, the sweeter the sound. I felt honored to sing alongside her.

As always, things moved more quickly than I would have liked. Within days of arriving in Ohio, I was singing on the Cathedral of Tomorrow's televised services. Thousands of people packed the church, and thousands more were watching around the country. Our group was there not to entertain or to sell a product, but to add to the worshipful atmosphere of the service.

I had been singing gospel music all my life, had been active in church, and had been at the heart of a publishing industry that printed hymnals filled with inspired lyrics, yet until that moment I don't think I fully understood what it meant to be a committed Christian. The more services I was a part of, the more Sunday school classes I attended, and the more I spoke with Rex Humbard, the more convinced I became that what I was looking for in life was not a chance to sing gospel music, but rather an opportunity to let God use gospel music to bring people to him.

Singing with the Weatherfords enhanced my own new feelings about worshiping God with my music. Earl and Lily Fern were good honest people who would not "sell" their music. They were Christians before they were performers, and as such they were excellent role models for me. Their lives were a ministry. Still, they worked me hard.

Each morning I had to get out of bed before dawn and drive for more than an hour up the road to Cleveland to do a live television show. The program went on the air at 7:00 and was a lot more difficult to pull off than early-morning radio had been. Each day it was an adventure, a grind, and a battle.

For starters, to do television we had to look good. We had to appear as sharp each morning as when we sang at church services. It was a huge challenge to get up early, ride in a cramped car for more than an hour, and then face the hot lights and cameras looking fresh and alive. Most mornings I felt anything but!

It was also extremely difficult to come up with new songs and arrangements each day. Since we couldn't do the same show over and over, we had to rehearse every day for hours just to get enough material for the next day's program. Because it was television, we couldn't cheat. On the radio we could read from a songbook, but in front of cameras we had to have the words down pat.

To make matters worse, being in good voice every day so early in the morning was almost impossible. Television's hot lights seemed to cook our throats and lungs. Cleveland's cold winter temperatures made the switch to the hot studio even more difficult.

On Friday and Saturday evenings we often hit the road, performing in churches throughout Ohio, Pennsylvania, and Indiana. The crowds that came to hear us knew us through television. They not only wanted to meet us in person, but wanted to have some of our records to take home. That meant I found myself in the recording studio almost as soon as I arrived in Akron. It was a great time in my life but was happening so fast that I barely had time to enjoy it.

I was content in the church, thrilled with the professionalism and commitment of the Weatherfords, and happy with my coworkers. Yet as I faced that first winter's cold winds, my thoughts often returned to Texas and my parents. When that happened, the old doubts rushed in. Dad was still not doing well. It would take a long time and a number of operations for him to get back on his feet. With each letter from home, I felt a bit guiltier about being so far away. Even though I felt the Lord's hand on my work and knew that I was growing spiritually as never before, I think I eventually might have left the Weatherfords and gone back home if God hadn't answered one of my mother's prayers.

I had come to Ohio for a job and had discovered so much more. As I studied my Bible and attended prayer groups, I had grown to the point where I was tithing for the first time in my life. Everywhere I looked I found someone who inspired me to do more and reach deeper. I felt fulfilled as never before. As if all this wasn't enough reason to stay, there was the choir—the most impressive choir I had ever heard. Yet what impressed me more than just their body of voices was one pretty, young member whose presence touched me each time I saw her.

In Ohio I didn't have any problem finding dates. Not long after arriving I purchased a brand new 1957 Chevy. Girls went crazy over the car. After church plenty of young ladies rode with me to grab a bite to eat. Yet it was the one who chose to ride in her own car that intrigued me. I simply couldn't get her out of my mind.

I was an old bachelor who had become set in my ways before I met VanLua Harris. She was ten years my junior and should have had better things to do than spend time with an old hick from Texas—and for a while it looked like she did. A lot of girls were taken by me simply because I was a singer, but not VanLua. She didn't throw herself at me like some of the others; rather, she was polite and refined. I figured she believed that I was a cad, but for some reason, whenever I got together with a church group for worship or fellowship, she was there.

One night I decided to follow her and make her notice me. When she stopped at a red light, I pulled up beside her and asked if she would come with me for a Coke. She declined and drove on. Humiliated, I followed along behind her. At the next light she offered me a second chance. Waving me to come beside her, she informed me that we could share a Coke but that she would drive. She wasn't going to get in my car; she didn't know me well enough.

That first Coke led to several others, and I soon discovered that I had never met anyone like VanLua. She was pretty, graceful, and talented, but more than all those things, she was bright. We could talk for hours about anything, and we often did. I experienced feelings like I had never felt before, and I scared myself by even thinking about marriage. For months VanLua and I visited, shared goals and dreams, and became best friends. For a man who had always been painfully shy, revealing this much of myself was remarkable. I am not even sure that Van realized the miracle she had created.

Still I was moving slowly as I was unsure of my feelings—that is, until another gospel group came to our church and one of their members asked Van for a date. I came unglued. I called her at work and at home every day just to make sure she wasn't seeing someone else. I'm sure she knew she had me hooked!

Wayne Jones, our assistant pastor, had been watching my feeble attempts to woo Van for months. He finally told me, "Son, if you don't intend to marry that girl, you had better go back to Texas now!" I guess my lovesickness was obvious to everyone but me!

In August, after more than a half year of just visiting, we kind of fell into dating. By October I asked her to marry me, and she finally decided that she could ride in my car!

Rex, his wife, Maude Aimee, and other friends were thrilled. They thought we were the perfect couple. Rex even wanted to marry us at the cathedral. I thought that was a wonderful idea—that is, until I found out about Rex's vision for our ceremony. He thought we should be married on the Sunday morning telecast with tens of thousands of viewers getting to watch one of the featured singers exchanging vows with a choir member. I was just a small-town boy who didn't know what to think of a wedding becoming an event, but over the next few weeks, Rex and my bride-to-be convinced me that it was the way to go.

On November 30, 1957, with 3,500 members of our congregation in attendance and the television cameras rolling, I sang "Because" as VanLua walked down the aisle of a beautifully decorated auditorium. As I watched her come toward me, I knew that I had never seen anyone as beautiful.

What a wedding it was. Our bridal party consisted of Earl and Lily Fern and Armond Morales. Henry Slaughter played the organ, and a wonderful choral group led by Audrey Mae Meir sang "I Love You Truly." Maude Aimee sang "Whither Thou Goest." After Van-Lua and I exchanged vows, Rex preached on families and commitment and I vowed to the Lord to take care of this woman for as long as I lived. When Rex gave his altar call, my new father-in-law came forward. I was overwhelmed that our marriage had opened a door for the Lord to come into this man's heart.

Though nine inches of snow covered the ground, I thought it was spring as we raced from the church to a reception at the Mayflower Hotel. Life couldn't get any better than this.

My mother was thrilled beyond words. She realized that by giving me up, her prayers had been answered. I was going to have a loving wife and a wonderful Christian home. If I had ignored the call from Earl Weatherford, I probably would have missed out on these blessings.

After a short honeymoon, Van and I set up housekeeping in a small rented home just outside of Akron. I may have been set in my ways, but my new bride seemed to have little trouble readjusting my thought process. Soon she had me trained better than most men who had been married twenty years. The strangest thing about it was that I didn't even realize I was being trained.

As our marriage blossomed, the Weatherfords blossomed as well. In January we lost our piano player but never missed a beat. I told Earl that I knew of a great keyboard player in Oklahoma who had recently played at our wedding. I tracked down my old Ozark Quartet buddy, Henry Slaughter, and within two weeks, Henry was in Akron accompanying us.

In 1958 Rex dedicated his new worship center, the Cathedral of Tomorrow. More than 6,500 people showed up that first Sunday morning and every week thereafter. Rex's ministry was exploding, and the Weatherfords were in greater demand than ever. The old Cadillac that had transported us to our performances was traded in for a touring bus. For the first time in my life, when I went down the road, I could sleep almost as well as I did at home. By fall I found that some nights I could even sleep better on the bus.

Our first child was born on September 15, 1959. She was the most beautiful little girl I had ever seen, so small and delicate that when I first held her in my arms I thought I might break her. Yet when she opened her mouth and cried, I realized that Carla was indeed a strong child. Many nights her strength kept us awake until the wee hours of the morning.

Fatherhood was a real change for me since I had never even considered what it would be like to have a child. But now that Carla was here, I couldn't imagine life without a little one to hold, nurture, and watch grow. Every day was filled with new surprises. And thanks to my steady work with the Weatherfords, there were very few anxieties about providing for her.

As I went shopping for Carla's first Christmas present, I knew my life was now complete. I was happy in my church, my marriage, and my family. I loved my work, had wonderful friends, and was growing spiritually. At home in Texas my father was making great strides and was back at his job. My mother had now realized that I had made the decision that was not just right for me, but for all of us. I couldn't imagine things getting any better, nor would I have been greedy enough to pray they would. Yet they did anyway.

The Weatherfords had become so well known that Chet Atkins and RCA asked us to record an album in Nashville. The recording that all of us had done in the past had been produced in the most modest of surroundings. None of us had ever even come close to trying anything as professional as Chet had set up. We soon discovered that the right producer and studio made a huge difference in the quality of the final product.

We recorded "In the Garden" in February 1959. I had never been so proud of a project in my life. Along with the title cut, we included our versions of "Footprints of Jesus," "One God," "House of Gold," "When I'm Walking in the Garden," and five more classic cuts. Thanks to the team that put it together, "In the Garden" became one of the best-received gospel albums of the era, marking the pinnacle of the Weatherfords' work.

With our financial status improving each year, Van and I could afford to stretch our wings and fly into middle-class life. In 1960 we bought a three-bedroom house in Stow, Ohio. It was modest, but it was new and all ours. A few months after we moved into our new home, we welcomed a son, Todd, into the nursery. Needless to say, we were proud to have a son to carry on the Payne name, and what a precious child he was. Now my life was filled with two small reasons to celebrate each day. No longer did I have to look very far to witness the miracle of life and love in action. Yet while I was celebrating being a father, I became aware that my wife had her work cut out for her with two babies only seventeen months apart and me away so much. It had to have been love, excitement, and faith that carried her through these times.

The next few years became a blur of Sunday morning services, recording dates, live performances, and television shows. Yet a few things did stand out. In 1961 I was at the National Quartet Convention in Memphis when a man approached me.

"You're with the Weatherfords, aren't you?" he asked.

"Yes," I replied. "My name is Glen Payne."

"Did you sing on the 'In the Garden' album?" the young man inquired.

"Yes, I did," I proudly answered.

"That is a classic, sir," Elvis Presley told me. "That album is one of my favorites. It is one of the best that has ever been done."

As Elvis walked over to the side of the stage to catch another performing quartet, I thought back to the time I had first watched him work. Little did I know he would have such a tremendous impact on the music world, nor did I imagine my music would ever impact him. As I would find out later from friends such as Larry Gatlin and Jake Hess, a lot of what we had done touched Elvis very deeply.

To have some of the biggest names in the world of music as fans, to be at the center of the largest weekly television ministry in the world, and to have more bookings than could be fulfilled, would have satisfied most people. I know that I was thrilled. But in spite of all this success, Earl Weatherford was getting antsy. I think that he thought the Weatherfords were losing their identity by being so closely aligned with Rex Humbard. In the spring of 1963, with hardly any warning, Earl announced that he and Lily Fern were moving to California. He invited me and the other members of the quartet to come along with them.

I couldn't begin to repay Earl for all I owed him. He had given me a chance when I was down and out, and he had treated me well. Working with the Weatherfords had led to the greatest spiritual growth of my life. Yet the very reasons I owed Earl so much were the reasons I couldn't go with him. Faced with no job, no income, and an uncertain future for the first time in years, I was going to stay in Ohio where I at least had friends, a family, and some roots. I was determined to make a go of it here. I didn't understand why I needed to stay, I just did!

chapter sixteen

HARD TIMES

Rex Humbard's deal had been with the Weatherfords. When Earl pulled out, Danny Koker, Bobby Clark, and I were set adrift. Though we wanted to stay with the Cathedral of Tomorrow, we had no contract or position with the church. Quickly the three of us had to come up with some answers.

Rex advised us to simply keep singing as a trio. He assured us that he would put us on salary in the fall if we developed. For the next three months, we would have to find work just to make ends meet. Our prospects weren't bright. I was deeply concerned as I had a wife and two small children to support and didn't have enough money in the bank to cover expenses for three months. The other guys were in the same boat. We all knew that if we didn't find work as a trio immediately, there would be no trio at all. Unless we stuck together, none of us would be able to cash in on Rex's promise for work in the fall.

As soon as Earl drove his bus out of Akron, Danny, Bobby, and I got on the phone and tried to "sell" ourselves as a trio to just about every church, pastor, and booker in the region. From the beginning, we faced a huge problem. No one had ever heard of the Cathedral Trio, and we didn't have a radio or television show or record albums to help push us. Most importantly, it was quartets, not trios, that were usually associated with gospel music. As a result, "Sorry" and "No thanks" were the usual responses we heard day after day.

At some point, the three of us decided to assign a week to each person. It was the responsibility of that person to find several places for us to perform during "his" week. In theory this division of power sounded good. In practice it was a bust. None of us found much of anything, and our bills kept piling up.

It only took me a couple of weeks without work to realize that I needed to roll up my sleeves and get on the phone with everyone I had ever met. My efforts secured a few engagements but no guaranteed money.

Those first dates were mainly at small churches in Ohio and Pennsylvania. Though we sounded good and were well received, the fact that we were an unknown commodity worked against us at each venue. Those who came to see us were the same folks who came to church whenever the doors were open. Because the crowds were small and poor, the love offerings to help cover our expenses often didn't even pay for our gasoline. With each passing week, it became harder to see how we were going to survive until September.

To bring in extra cash, I searched high and low for every record, publicity photograph, and anything else that might have a bit of commercial appeal at our performances. Even though I found people willing to buy my merchandise at bargain-basement prices, I had only a limited supply to sell.

As July melted into August in the summer of 1963, I felt heat like never before—the pressure of trying to keep Danny, Bobby, and me together as a group until the fall. I was working myself to the bone but only spinning my wheels. Things got so bad that we began appearing at three places each Sunday. After a morning service, we would load up and drive down the road for an afternoon service and then sing at another church at night. By the end of the day, we would carefully count the money we had taken in. If it didn't total more than a hundred dollars, we knew we were in trouble. More often than not, it didn't.

The only thing sustaining us besides working frantically to make ends meet was our faith. We prayed for guidance at every stop and every turn. Hard work made it possible for us to eat, but it was prayer and faith that kept us together. Every time we seemed to reach the end of the road, a church would invite us to sing, and that would keep us going for one more week. Friends helped out, too, and we made it through until Rex put us on the payroll.

In the midst of a financial panic, my young wife had stayed calm. In Van's mind the house and car didn't matter that much anyway. Even if we lost them, we still had each other and the kids. We would get by, she reasoned, and then we would rebuild and come back stronger. How I leaned on her strength as I fought daily to keep my own.

While we had been on the road, I had not had the chance to attend Sunday school and had lost contact with many friends. When I finally was able to rejoin the people at church, I discovered that they hadn't lost contact with me or the trio. They had been praying for us every step of the way, keeping up with our needs, dreams, and heartbreaks. Without our realizing it, they had wrapped their arms of faith around us. How thankful I was to have this extended family supporting us with their love and care.

In hindsight, that summer was an important test for me, my family, and the others who made up our trio. It proved to us how committed we were to what we were doing. It was a test that would serve as a model for future suffering and survival as well. Without the summer of '63, I don't know if I could have ridden out the tough times we faced when we tried to take the Cathedral Quartet out on its own six years later.

Beginning in September, and for the next year, the Cathedral Trio became the official vocal group of the Cathedral of Tomorrow. The weekly telecasts gave us a platform to build on, and booking dates quickly accelerated, love offerings grew, and our reputation as gospel music singers flourished. With Danny singing baritone and playing piano, Bobby supplying the tenor, and me providing the lead, we were a solid ensemble. Audiences loved the way we sang old classics like "It Is No Secret" and "God Will Take Care of You." They also liked our interpretations of newer songs, such as Henry Slaughter's "The Answer Came." By sticking out the bad times, we had once again been granted the blessings of better times.

By the summer of 1964 we had almost forgotten how hungry we had been the year before. Things were almost as stable as they had been with the Weatherfords. Nevertheless, I sensed something missing from my life and from the group.

I had grown up with the Stamps' music style presented and performed by quartets. Four men singing four parts and blending as one voice—that's the way I had always believed gospel music sounded best. No matter how good the Cathedral Trio was, I looked longingly at groups like the Statesmen and Blackwoods and wished we could generate their full sound.

I had no idea that Rex Humbard was also missing the depth provided by true quartet sounds. While he liked the Cathedral Trio, he was a man who liked to shake things up a bit as long as the shaking was done to enhance Christian growth. He must have had this in mind when he approached Bobby, Danny, and me in November.

"Guys," he began, "you have really developed a good sound. I am proud you're with me. The Cathedral Trio adds so much to the worshipful atmosphere of our services. Yet I believe we can make your little group even better. Gentlemen," he continued, "I think it would be good if you were to expand into a quartet. I really believe it would add quality to your group as well as provide our congregation and television audience with something they would really love. There is just something special about quartet music, and I think we all know it."

We all pretended to consider Rex's idea for a few minutes as though it were a new one for us, but we could hardly hold back our enthusiasm. Still we wondered how we would find the right man for the job.

Danny, Bobby, and I had each worked with some really good bass singers. We knew a handful of men who could add a wonderful new dimension to our group, but they were already employed by other quartets. We doubted that any of them would leave to come to Ohio. Danny was especially sold on one man he had teamed with in the past. But like all the others, this singer was firmly anchored to one of the nation's better-known quartets.

Like Danny, Rex's line of thought turned to the same singer they had both known in the past. While Danny seemed convinced the man wouldn't leave the Blue Ridge Quartet, Rex felt we needed to contact him anyway. He made the call that day.

Danny and I nearly fell over when Rex casually remarked that the bass singer of the Blue Ridge Quartet would be arriving soon to fill the void. While both Danny and Bobby were elated, I was a bit more reserved. I had heard him sing on records and radio and liked his sound, but unlike the others, I didn't know him personally. I knew it was easier to find a good singer than to find a good man to have by your side day in and day out. I prayed he would be right for our group.

Over the course of the next year, I would welcome two new members to my family. Van and I welcomed our daughter Darla in September. This darling bundle with chubby cheeks, upturned nose, and dark eyes completed our home; but by the time this beautiful, little girl arrived, I already knew that George Younce was not just a great bass singer, he was my brother too. I prayed he would stay with the Cathedral Quartet for a long time.

PART THREE

George and Glen, 1950

The Cathedrals

chapter seventeen

WE ARE THE
CATHEDRAL QUARTET

SOME MOMENTS IN LIFE stand out clearly no matter how much time has elapsed. November 1964 held such a moment for me, when I first walked into the Cathedral of Tomorrow and introduced myself to the three men who had invited me to help them make the Cathedral Trio a quartet. It was a quiet but electric event, one of the turning points in my life.

I knew Danny Koker from my first stint in Ohio with the Weatherfords, but I didn't know how a decade of time had changed him. He may have changed even as much as had Rex Humbard's church. My how it had grown! When I left, Rex's church had been in a smaller building, the services had been broadcast only on radio, and the church's fame had been regional. Now the congregation met in the largest worship hall I had ever seen, services were broadcast coast to coast on television, and Rex was probably the best-known preacher in the country with the exception of Billy Graham. As I opened the door to my new professional home, once again I felt like a country boy.

All my fears about the new job jumped out the window as soon as Glen Payne spotted me. I recognized him immediately from seeing him at concerts. Still I didn't really "know" the man, nor did I know how he might react to me as a team member. When he smiled and crossed the room to shake my hand, the heaviness that had clouded the moment evaporated. I knew I was in the right place. As he introduced himself and we stared eye to eye, I realized that this job had been God-ordained. Glen's handshake and manner made me feel so comfortable that it seemed like I had known him all my life. Bobby and Danny were the same. These guys weren't going to test me or keep me at arm's length during a probationary period; they were too excited about putting a quartet together.

Clara and I had been happy and comfortable in Spartanburg. Our kids loved it there. Even more than I, Clara was concerned that a new city, new church, and new environment just wouldn't be right for us. How I wished that she had been with me to meet Glen, Bobby, and Danny that first day. I felt sure she would have known everything was going to be all right. But Clara was still at home in Spartanburg. I had come by myself to find a home for us and had searched several neighborhoods before spotting the right one on a quiet tree-lined street. It nearly called out to me as I walked up the steps.

A few days later, I brought Clara to Ohio and to the house I had already arranged to purchase. I didn't know how she would react. Still unnerved about picking up and moving so quickly, she opened the front door tentatively. Then I caught a sparkle in her eye and a smile on her face. She hadn't said a word, but I knew she felt at home too. My biggest prayer had been answered, and I could get on with the work at hand.

The first song I practiced and performed with the Cathedral Quartet was "I Know Who Holds Tomorrow." As that gospel classic moved over the congregation on that initial Sunday morning, I was struck by the incredible sound bouncing back to me. I was so caught up listening to the glorious blend of the other three voices that I almost quit singing my own part. I had spent over half my life singing gospel music and had sung with some pretty good groups, but I had never heard anything like this sound. It was more polished, fuller, and more spiritual than any music I had ever helped create with any other group. As I looked at Bobby, Danny, and Glen, I realized that they were sharing the same thing I was feeling. As excited as a child with a new toy, I didn't want the number to end.

Bobby Clark and Danny Koker each brought something special to our new group. Bobby was a tenor who didn't just hit a note—he captured it, held it, and made it his own. Danny was not only a fine baritone, but a great pianist and arranger. His inspiration served as the springboard from which so many of our unique arrangements were born. Yet as much as I admired these two talented men, I quickly realized that Glen was the one who made it all come together.

I had never worked with a lead singer like Glen. He was not only the best lead I had ever known, he was the most professional. He didn't just want to perform a song well, he wanted to do it perfectly; and his drive for perfection pulled us all up. That drive coupled with the man's extraordinary talents was why the Cathedral Quartet quickly developed a unique sound and one of the best blends in the world of southern gospel music. We all had our special abilities, but Glen was the anchor that held us in place.

As well as we got along together when we worked, Glen and I got along even better as friends. He was more reserved and organized, he didn't fool around as much and didn't crack as many jokes, but he put up with my foolishness and my teasing and even brought out a more serious side of me from time to time. No matter what we were doing, we enjoyed being together.

Clara and Van had a relationship like Glen's and mine. Our kids also became best friends. Whatever was going on in our children's lives, from Little League games to high school parties, made both the Paynes' and the Younces' personal calendars. We became an extended family.

It was also great to be with the Cathedral Quartet because we had so much time to practice. When I was with other quartets, we pretty much worked out our numbers during live shows. We just didn't have the time to spend on special arrangements. Now, because we were on the Humbard staff and usually only did outside performances on Saturday nights, we had plenty of time to practice every day. It was like going back to school. During the two hours of daily work, I was learning more about music, expanding my range, and becoming more professional in my presentation. I was also beginning to realize that a quartet could develop a sound that was fresh, alive, and unique.

Soon after we formed the quartet, Rex got us a deal with Benson Records. Once again my world expanded. In the past a recording session meant doing some songs as quickly as we could lay down the tracks. Now I was with a group that took recording to a new level. We brought in new concepts that had never been tried with quartet music. We added strings and brass, changed the arrangements of old standards, and tried to create a unique sound. It was a constantly evolving process that stretched the limits of what was expected from southern gospel, an intermixing of new ideas and an old sound combined with a professionalism usually reserved for the most successful pop acts.

Benson didn't know what to do with us. Almost everyone at the label thought we were a little crazy. When we wanted more than the other quartets, they were shocked. It wasn't that we didn't like the other groups; we just wanted to do our own thing. Back then, doing your own thing in gospel music was scary. Benson probably would have cut us loose had it not been for one thing: We sold records. Thanks to Rex's weekly telecasts and the fact that we could promote our records to millions via these programs, we were selling thousands of albums each week. Heaven knows what the Benson people were thinking as they kept pressing records that they thought were doomed to fail.

On Saturday nights the quartet would pile into a station wagon and roll off to New York, Philadelphia, or another large eastern city. In churches, large auditoriums, or civic centers we would perform for audiences numbering in the thousands. Usually a local quartet would open for us, then we would do an hour program. The Humbard telecasts had made us so universally known and accepted that we were even booked to work an African-American church convention at the height of the civil rights movement in the midst of race riots in many of America's inner cities! Gospel music seemed to be the key to opening any door or reaching any crowd.

In Pennsylvania we were surprised to discover young people turning out for us in large numbers. We even met one young man who formed his own quartet after hearing us. After that first meeting, this teenager would drive hours just to catch us. We never knew where he would show up next. Joe Bonsell of the Faith Four even convinced us to come back to his house in Philly so that his mother could feed us. Little did we know then that Joe would eventually find fame with the Oak Ridge Boys. We just thought he was a hyperactive kid who talked like a Yankee but had a deep devotion to southern gospel music.

It was such an exciting time for all of us. The world was opening up to gospel music as never before. No longer was interest limited to the rural South. We could go anywhere and did.

The only negative aspect of having Saturday night gigs was that we always had to be back in Akron for Rex's Sunday morning services. This meant driving all night, getting into Ohio just after sunup, showering, shaving, and appearing fresh when we went on the air. At first I didn't see any way we could manage this, but Glen made even this routine easy for the rest of us. While we slept, he would drive every mile of the trip back home. I would soon find out that no matter how much a person tried to do for Glen, he would always do more in return. I still owe him for things he did to make my life easier in 1965, which means that I am more than thirty years behind on payback.

Besides our Saturday night concerts, the only other time we got out on the road was during Rex's rallies. He had a plane and would fly us all over the nation for crusade-type events. With his Sunday morning broadcasts on more than 350 stations, we were appearing with a man who was not only well known, but loved and respected. Thousands filled stadiums and arenas wherever we went. I couldn't believe the response we got each time we sang. It was like nothing I had ever heard in all my years of performing.

By 1966 I thought we had it made. Our records were selling well, I had what amounted to a job with normal hours, and I was doing what I loved. We had even traveled to the Holy Land and recorded an album, the first American music group to do so. How powerfully moving it was to sing "Up from the Grave He Arose" while standing in Christ's tomb. We recorded "The Old Rugged Cross" on Palm Sunday and sang "In the Garden" while we were in the Garden of Gethsemane. I couldn't have counted my blessings had I tried. There were just too many!

Glen and I both figured that things would never change. We just assumed that the Lord had put us in this place to stay. And why wouldn't we want to always stay here? We traveled in style. We ate steaks. We worked with the finest musicians and in the nicest studios. And best of all, we got to spend time with our wives, be with our children for all their important events, teach Sunday school classes, and live like normal people. What a joy it was for a quartet singer to be "normal."

I was having so much fun being a full-time father to our two latest arrivals, Tara and George Lane, that at times I forgot that being a dad was supposed to be work. Because of our arrangement with the

Cathedrals, I could be something of a Mr. Mom a generation before the term was invented. I met my older daughter's boyfriends, puzzled over my girls' homework, and even got to go shopping with them. Few men of this era could have had this kind of life. Yet I did, and so did Glen, Bobby, and Danny.

A number of people in the business were probably jealous of us. They thought of us as part-timers, yet financially we were doing better than they were. We spent time with our wives and kids, and they barely knew theirs. We had a home life; they lived on a bus. I knew a bunch of quartets that gladly would have traded places with us. Yet what we didn't realize was that the very thing that was feeding us and making our lives so easy during this time would soon come back to haunt us.

By 1968 Bobby Clark felt an urge to move on. He had begun to feel a bit trapped by simply being a singer and thought the Lord wanted him to do more with his talents. After much struggling, he traded his "easy" life for full-time Christian service as a preacher at a church in Florida.

Danny Koker was also feeling a bit restricted by the quartet format. He wanted to become more involved in direct and daily evangelism. After much prayer, Danny left our group to work with choral music.

Glen and I hated to see these guys leave. We knew their talents were rare and that replacing them would be all but impossible. Yet even more we hated losing Bobby and Danny's close friendship. We could always replace a singer, but brothers were harder to come by.

To fill the gaps, we hired two young men we had gotten to know during one of Rex's rallies. George Amon Webster and Mack Taunton had both been born in Arkansas but had migrated to the Midwest in their youth. They had a strong background in gospel music and had performed with local quartets but weren't nearly as seasoned as the men whose shoes they had to fill. To give the boys time to mature, Glen and I took on additional responsibilities with the quartet and became teachers and mentors too.

Danny had always been our master of ceremonies, the man who introduced everyone, kept the shows moving, and made the jokes. Suddenly those duties fell to me. On my first night, I couldn't even remember everyone's name. When it came time to introduce one young man who was playing guitar for Rex's orchestra, I came up blank. It took me a long time to find my way and feel comfortable as the man out front.

Since Glen was a much better musician than I, he took over a lot of the arranging and instructing duties. Though he was more equipped and prepared for his new jobs than I was, it even took this clever veteran a few weeks to get his legs under him. The transition was anything but smooth. Still, Glen and I both knew we had a sweet deal. What we didn't know was that the deal was about to sour a little.

After a few months, the new edition of the Cathedral Quartet was still not nearly as good as the original. We were all working hard, but it was taking awhile to develop a solid blend. George and Mack were going to be all right, but they still had a way to go before fully realizing the trademark Cathedral sound. Yet because we had an ideal working and learning situation, we weren't concerned about the time it was going to take.

Each day we met at the church and practiced for a couple of hours. George and Mack were not just growing into their parts, they were also beginning to develop styles that would soon set them apart from Danny and Bobby. Given enough time, I knew the Cathedrals would come to their old standards. But time was not on our side.

As the years had passed and the Cathedral Quartet had become a more significant part of the Humbard organization, Rex had asked us to take over more and more duties at the church. I was involved in the mail order business, and Glen had become the organization's booker for rallies as well as the man who found hotel accommodations, arranged catering, and made travel arrangements. Since we had plenty of time for these business chores, we didn't mind. When our duties were expanded into counseling-type work, however, Glen and I both began to feel very uncomfortable.

We believed the Lord called people to counsel with others about personal matters, and we simply didn't feel called. Rex needed people who felt comfortable in this role, so we began to wonder if we weren't being led to take our ministry in a new direction, allowing Rex to bring someone in who could do whatever his growing ministry needed.

For months we prayed about whether to expand our work with Rex or leave and go out on our own. If Danny and Bobby had still been with us, the answer would have been far easier. The original group had a fully developed sound strong enough to play on the road. But Glen and I knew we were still a few months away from developing that complete package with George and Mack. Not only would it be hard for the two of us to leave the security of the cathedral for the road, it would be doubly hard on the two new guys. They would be forced to learn on the fly, immediately performing a lot of things they simply hadn't had the time to master. As we stumbled forward unable to do everything Rex hoped we could, we knew a decision had to be made.

Almost everyone we knew told us to do whatever Rex asked and stay hooked to a sure thing. This looked like the reasonable thing to do, but it wouldn't have been honest. Glen and I knew the Lord had called us to sing his music. Doing something we weren't called to do would not only hurt us, but would hurt God's work too. Finally, even though we realized the world was going to think we were crazy, we took the biggest step of faith we would ever take. We decided to leave the Cathedral of Tomorrow and hit the road like a normal quartet.

Rex couldn't have been more supportive. He not only encouraged us, but informed his audiences that they would soon be able to see us in person. With his support, we thought that our transition from being a part of the Humbard group to an independent entity would be a much easier road than most new groups had to travel when they tried to carve out an audience and an identity for themselves. It didn't take long to find out that any previous association we had had with Rex, Benson, or anyone else really didn't matter at all.

Our last rally with the Humbard group took us to Canada. More than eight thousand people filled a hall that night and clapped enthusiastically for our quartet work. In the parking lot, a local promoter was proudly placing announcements under each car's windshield wiper, trumpeting the fact that the Cathedral Quartet would be coming back in a few weeks for a full concert of music. With the reception we received that night, we assumed our launch into independence would be a triumphant one. When we returned to that same concert hall in Canada a few weeks later, it was a moment to remember. I can see it now as clearly as I did that night almost thirty years ago: As we walked onto the stage, we saw over 7,700 empty chairs and only 300 faintly curious ticket buyers waiting for us to sing. I even wondered whether we had walked out on the right night. As it turned out, this would be one of the better audiences to see the Cathedral Quartet in 1968.

chapter eighteen

AFTER A LIFETIME OF WORK— BEGINNING AGAIN

THAT FIRST DATE we worked in Canada foreshadowed what was to come. We had just arrived when I slipped on the ice and fell. The second I hit I knew I had broken my wrist. Yet despite George's urging that I take care of it, I tried to brush it off. This was our first concert as an independent group, and I couldn't afford to do anything to mess it up. Rather than go to the hospital and get my wrist set, I took a couple of aspirin and tried to ignore the pain.

For the next few years the Cathedral Quartet had to ignore pain a lot. Though we knew we were doing God's will, it was still tough to go on night after night when no one really seemed to notice us.

The trouble was that we were as green as grass and really weren't that good when we started out on our own. When we left Rex's church, we lost not only our weekly telecast and paychecks, but our record deal and our forum for generating bookings. Counting that first show in Canada that had twenty times more empty seats than paying customers, we had three dates in our books for all of 1970 when we headed out to test the waters.

We had assumed that at least a part of Rex's audience would follow us in our move. Yet for reasons none of us understood at first, they didn't. Even though I didn't fully comprehend why we had been so quickly forgotten, I began to realize that our easy life over the last few years was now working against us. No one seemed to realize that we were a full-time quartet. It was as if we had just been a part of Rex's choir, nothing more. Therefore, few took us seriously when we were away from the venue we had once called home. Discovering that was almost as painful as finding out just how badly I had broken my wrist.

After getting my shattered bones set, I got on the phone and began calling everyone I knew, looking for places to play. As I faced rejection after rejection, I began to feel as though I had been caught in some kind of time machine. It was like replaying the three-month nightmare I had experienced with the Cathedral Trio before Rex put us on the payroll. Only this time there was no promise of a future paycheck. After the first three lean months, the only thing we had to look forward to was three more lean months. That was frightening.

Compounding our business problems as a quartet was the fact that George and I had pressing personal problems as well. Both his father and my mother were ill. We each had to travel great distances on a moment's notice to be with our families in North Carolina and Texas. At the very time we should have been devoting ourselves to our profession, we couldn't. For a while, it seemed that everything was working against us. Yet neither of us was going to cheat his family in favor of the business, not after all our parents had done for us over the years.

George was extremely close to his father. His dad was proud that his son had become a gospel singer, and it was immensely hard to watch the man who had been so supportive of his life and career go downhill. On our long drives to shows, the two of us often talked about our feelings, and I got an even clearer picture of the man who had so influenced my friend's lifestyle, morals, and even his bass voice. I began to feel as if I were losing a father and mentor too.

While George's father was dying, my mother was suffering a slow, painful death from cancer. How I wished that I could do something, anything, to ease her pain. But now I couldn't even bring her good news about my work. I could only hold her hand, talk about old times, and share my love.

George lost his father and I lost my mother at about the same time. Both of us were so broke we had to borrow money to fly home for the funerals. Their deaths added to the depression that surrounded us at every turn. It made the sense of loss greater and the hurt that much deeper.

It would have made sense to give up. Promoters couldn't book dates for us, most of the places I found couldn't offer enough to pay for our expenses, and nobody was interested in giving us a record deal. Yet even when our bank accounts had been drained and we were wondering how long the bald tires on the wagon would hold out, we always managed to find something positive to hang on to. I would be feeling down, and George would crack a joke or tell a funny story. Just when things seemed hopeless, the Lord would provide us with an audience that appreciated and encouraged us. I would be looking for inspiration and find it in a song. No matter how bad things got, there always seemed to be a rainbow just ahead.

At home our wives and kids were tremendous. I asked them time and again whether they wanted me to quit. Despite having to give up things that had always been a part of their lives, wearing clothing until it wore out or it was badly out of style, and not seeing their father for weeks on end as I traveled to small churches around the country, they would hear nothing of my giving up. They told me to stick it out. They believed in me and in the Cathedrals. Their faith carried me along the rough ride.

On those long trips to churches in towns that weren't even on the map, George and I often stayed awake talking about our wives and families. We couldn't believe that they were willing to shoulder so much of the anguish of having us reestablish ourselves. We also were amazed by their faith. This helped us realize that what we were doing was more than a job—it was a mission.

During that first hungry year, George, George Amon, Mack, and I rededicated ourselves to ministering with our music. We no longer saw ourselves as entertainers who sang gospel songs; rather, we had responded to a call to use our talents in service and evangelism. With that clarified sense of purpose, it became far easier to lose money at a small church and still give the few who had gathered everything we had. The more we dedicated each performance to Christ, the happier and more satisfied we became with our work.

George Amon and Mack really began to grow during this period. They began to develop the confidence and bearing that mark first-rate singers. The blend that had once been neither strong nor tight, was starting to sound "big" and smooth. And that professional sound eventually got us noticed. We received invitations to sing in larger venues and began to see a small light at the end of the tunnel.

W. B. Nowlin, one of the top bookers in the Southwest and an old friend from my days with the Stamps, was one of the first to take a big chance on us. His "Battle of Song" concerts featured some of the top names in the business. Thousands would gather in places like Oklahoma City, Fort Worth, Houston, and San Antonio to hear the likes of the Blackwoods, the Statesmen, the Happy Goodmans, and the Speers. Into this environment W. B. not only invited us, but paid us as equals.

The Nowlin shows offered a chance for us to display our wares as well as gave us a forum for measuring ourselves against the best groups in gospel music. At first our sound, though improving, was not as polished as the top groups. And while we offered a few tapes and records that we had produced ourselves in a bargain-basement recording studio, they were offering a catalog of merchandise that was backed by the big labels. While we pulled up to the first few dates in a station wagon and then later in a tiny, old motor home we called the egg crate, they showed up in big, long buses that had staterooms, stereos, and televisions. Though we were simply outclassed at every turn, W. B. never mentioned it and continued booking us over the objections of others who thought we weren't ready.

One night in Oklahoma City we watched other groups sell hundreds of records and tapes after the show while we managed to find three people to buy ours. The next morning one of the ladies who had bought our album brought it back to us for a refund. It seems that she had confused us with another group. I am surprised that we had the five dollars to give back to her, because that morning we had eaten a big breakfast. We laughed about that refund as we got back into the egg crate, but it really was just another episode in a very humbling time.

Christmas was lean for our families that year. Nevertheless, it wasn't a sad time. We had at least broken even, developed a much stronger sound, and had grown in our commitment, spirit, and resolve. We now had a sound that, while not perfect, was something of which everyone could be proud.

In that initial year, George Amon Webster had written such wonderful songs as "He Loves Me" and "Thanks for Loving Me." Whenever we sang them, people were moved by the performance and the message.

During this time, George Younce also had composed a hauntingly beautiful song of Christian commitment called "Yesterday." We were reaching hearts and souls with "Statue of Liberty," "I'll Have a New Life," and a new Bill Gaither composition, "Gentle Shepherd." Our audiences, though still small, were beginning to respond in ways that made our mission of reaching souls for Christ come alive. Though no longer involved in the large Humbard rallies, we discovered in those first years that the Lord works just as powerfully in small groups. We weren't spinning our wheels; we were just serving the Lord one life at a time. And those lives began to add up.

We usually ended our programs with the old classic "Everybody Will Be Happy over There." This song spoke volumes about the way George, the other guys, and I felt about the Cathedral Quartet. Things were tough, but in time we would be enjoying eternal happiness and peace. This knowledge helped us go the distance.

By 1970 our sound had improved enough that Word Records in Waco, Texas, decided to give us a shot at recording again. They put us on their Canaan label, and we were deeply appreciative. Management quickly grew to love the way we sounded in the studio and in concert. Yet our product gathered more dust than profits. After a couple of albums that didn't sell well, they should have cut us loose, but they didn't. Like W. B. Nowlin, they stuck with us, figuring that eventually we would find an audience.

We added an old friend, Haskell Cooley, to our group as a piano player. Financially this didn't make much sense. Having another mouth to feed didn't seem smart, but we wanted to free up George Amon to join us at the microphone. Adding Haskell allowed him to concentrate on singing, making us look more like a standard gospel quartet.

In the midst of our slow building process, the Blackwoods called George Younce. J. D. Sumner, their longtime bass singer, had bought the rights to the Stamps Quartet name and was restarting the quartet. The Blackwoods wanted George to quit us and join them as their bass. George was the best possible choice for the job. Logic told him to accept, because the Blackwoods were on top of the gospel world.

They had tradition, heritage, history, and a huge fan base, and they were offering him a sweet deal. George, however, didn't listen to logic; he listened to his heart and stayed with us.

To this day I don't know why a man would choose suffering and lack of a guaranteed income over success and prosperity, but I'm so glad George did. Losing him probably would have meant losing the Cathedrals. He was that large a force with our small legion of fans. Without his voice, wit, charm, and friendship, I would have been hard-pressed to continue. Thankfully, I never had to find out if I could have gone on without my best friend.

As we continued our uphill battle, members of the quartet sometimes got pretty discouraged. I didn't blame them. For a while, the membership of the Cathedrals was pretty liquid. Haskell Cooley, for instance, left us and was replaced by Lorne Matthews at the piano. Yet we still kept going and improving.

Finally, we socked away enough money from concession sales to purchase an old bus. This made travel much easier. Still, when we pulled in next to the big quartets, we didn't measure up. Our vehicles may have been the same length now, but our careers were on far different levels.

During the early seventies, we released some good albums, such as *Somebody Loves Me*, *A Little Bit of Everything*, and *Welcome to Our World*. The problem was that there just weren't enough people who were being welcomed into our world of music. We weren't generating a lot of airplay on gospel stations, nor were we selling out concerts in big markets. We seemed a little better off every year, but we still had a long way to go to fight our way back to where we had been when we were a featured part of the Cathedral of Tomorrow. A lot of people thought we would never get there.

Herman Harper, one of the original Oak Ridge Boys who had quit singing to become an agent, thought we had some potential, so he signed on to help book us through Don Light Talent in Nashville. Herman and the folks at Don Light worked hard, but it didn't take them long to discover something of which we were already painfully aware. The Cathedral Quartet was a group people turned to when they couldn't get the Blackwoods, Imperials, Speers, Statesmen, Goodmans, or Stamps.

By the early seventies, about the only day of the week we were ever home was Monday. That was the one day George and I reintroduced ourselves to our families and tried to catch up on our busy-work. For two men who had once been privileged to take their children to school and to attend almost every Little League game, we found ourselves out of touch. This was the hardest part of keeping the Cathedrals going.

On a snowy winter night in 1973, our bus skidded on the ice just outside of Staunton, Virginia. In what many may have viewed as a sign from Providence, the old silver beast fell on its side and rolled down a huge hill. In what had to have been a miracle, we managed to pull ourselves out of the twisted wreckage with no injuries. Yet as we surveyed the damage to our totaled bus, we had to wonder if it was worth it to keep going. Was losing precious time with our loved ones and taking chances on snow-covered roads what the Lord really had in mind for us?

As I stared at what was left of our once-proud means of transportation, I was touched with a sense of irony. Our journey had begun on a snowy night in Canada, where a patch of ice had caused me to fall and break my wrist. Now, thousands of miles and four years away from that disappointing beginning, a patch of ice had brought us crashing down once again. Would we get up, brush ourselves off, and keep going, or would we finally give up and try something else? None of us knew for sure at that moment.

chapter nineteen

A TASTE
OF SUCCESS

COMPETITION IS RAMPANT in gospel music. Naturally, each group wants a number-one record and a Dove Award labeling them tops in their field. In the midst of hard-fought rivalries in the gospel music business, however, runs a spirit that is rare in other segments of the entertainment industry. Many of those whose living depends on selling more tickets and records than the next group are always watching out for others who are struggling to make ends meet. In our case, a lot of people at the top were reaching down to help us up on every step of our long journey.

One of those to whom Glen and I will always be grateful is Les Beasley of the Florida Boys. In the sixties and seventies, Les developed the *Gospel Singing Jubilee*, the most successful southern gospel music show on television. His efforts were rewarded largely because he ran a first-class show. He invested in color cameras and better sound systems long before many network shows went that route. He also used experienced talent behind the camera as well as in front of it. Quartets such as the Happy Goodmans, Imperials, Speer Family, and Blackwoods gave the *Jubilee* a gospel status equivalent to that of country music's Grand Ole Opry. This kind of star power made both the fans and advertisers happy. So it was understandable that in the early seventies when Les began to invite us, it didn't make many people happy. After all, who wanted a group that often had trouble *giving* away their records?

The *Jubilee* was a major-league show, and we were still a minor-league quartet. The other groups were drawing better and selling more. They also had a legion of hard-core fans. A lot of critics and fans alike thought that Glen's fame had probably peaked with the Weatherfords and mine with the Blue Ridge Quartet.

As a friend, Les would have been completely justified in giving us a couple of shots on his show and then moving on to someone else. As a businessman, he probably should have. Yet Les kept bringing us back even when viewers weren't clamoring for the Cathedrals. He believed in us and was willing to give us time to develop an audience.

Bill Gaither recently put together a video made up of many of the clips of us taken from the *Jubilee*. When you watch those strung-together segments, it is obvious that we were working very hard to succeed. In shot after shot, we can be seen with the latest styles, such as long sideburns, wide collars and ties, and in some cases, even double-knit suits. We thought we looked real sharp. In retrospect we were wrong about that. Yet as we progressed from year to year and appearance to appearance, one thing did come out: Musically we were getting better with each show.

It took awhile for gospel music fans to notice that in spite of our green leisure suits, our sound was maturing. By the mid seventies, many of these same people who had once used our segment to check out the other groups' record tables, were staying and listening to us sing. Without the *Jubilee* I don't know how long it would have taken us to catch on with the southern gospel crowd.

Even though the fans were beginning to listen to us in larger numbers, we still weren't tearing them up like the Goodmans. It was a humbling experience to follow this family on stage. They were so incredible that their fans would be worked up into a frenzy when they finished. When the Goodmans walked off the stage, we would peek from behind the curtain to see thousands shouting, screaming, and praising God. It really got me pumped up. What a great crowd! Yet when we walked out and sang for the same people, the response was polite applause.

Of course it wasn't Howard, Vestal, and Rusty Goodman's fault. The fans simply loved them and didn't want anyone else to share their stage. This singing family had discovered their own special sound and unique identity and had built on it for years. Their fans treasured their sincerity and honesty. In other words, they had what we wanted and couldn't seem to get.

We knew the Goodmans hadn't become popular overnight, and it certainly helped when they told us how they used to feel inadequate next to groups like the Blackwoods. Howard kept telling us that our day was coming; all we had to do was work hard, pray, and hang in there. I couldn't help wondering whether he was a better musician than forecaster of musical trends. It just didn't seem to me that "our day" was ever going to come.

One night when Howard was introducing us to an audience, he informed the Goodman fans that the Cathedrals were "easy on the ears but heavy in the spirit." At that point the fans began to listen to us a bit more closely and came to realize that we were a little bit different than everyone else. It was also around this time that we began to grasp our own identity as well. Our version of southern gospel wasn't just like the Florida Boys or the Stamps.

By 1975 our singing was becoming more and more identifiable, and we were beginning to be listened to more closely by people in and out of the industry. Though we still weren't tearing up the charts, we sensed that Howard was right: Times were changing, gospel music's influence was expanding beyond the South, and even though the rewards weren't coming yet, our fan base seemed to be growing larger and more loyal. We were now getting a lot of return customers, an indication that we were doing a good job with our stage presentation and our music.

The thing that makes me proudest is that we never knowingly shortchanged anyone. We gave our all even to congregations that didn't have enough money to pay our expenses. Fifty poor people in a small rural church got just as good a performance as did thousands in Oklahoma City. We felt that we were involved in a ministry and a mission. As a result, we prayed that each person who came to hear us might come to know Christ better through our music. Hence, we had tremendous spiritual blessings even when the offerings didn't seem so blessed.

We couldn't eat and pay bills on good feelings alone. So life offstage wasn't always as much fun as it was onstage. I would watch Glen study the books, and then after he showed me the numbers, we both would worry about how to pay the bills for one more month. Just about the time we thought we couldn't make it through another week, God would send an opportunity that would generate just enough funds to keep us going for one more day. I couldn't begin to count how many times these last-minute reprieves happened during our first ten years on our own. It just seemed that when we couldn't keep ourselves going; the Lord did it for us. So when things were at their worst, we had strong arms to hold our heads above the water.

Hard work and dedication always pay off in the long run. I know it did for the Cathedrals. Not only did we work nearly every day of the week, but we rehearsed hard too. During a two-hour slot before a show, we practiced sharpening our sound and blend as well as coming up with new arrangements. With Glen urging us on, we pushed to eliminate our weak points and to bring out a sound that was as smooth, sweet, and spiritual as Howard Goodman "thought" it already was. One of those who noticed our improving sound and dedication was the nation's hottest contemporary songwriter, Bill Gaither.

Glen had known Bill as far back as Glen's teaching days at the Stamps Singing School. Bill had also hung around a bit during Glen's stint with the Weatherfords. At that time Gaither was just a struggling young songwriter trying to get someone to record some of his compositions. A likeable young man with a lot of raw talent, he wasn't a man who seemed about to set the world of spiritual music on fire. Nevertheless, Glen always took the time to visit with Bill and encourage him. He never dreamed the boy would someday multiply that kindness back to him.

About the time I landed with the Cathedrals, Bill and his wife, Gloria, were building reputations as top-notch songwriters. I would see Bill at some of the small Indiana churches where we worked. Though I rarely got to visit with him, I always noticed him sitting in the back, where he seemed to be listening intently to everything we sang. As his own career took off with such great songs as "Because He Lives," "God Gave the Song," and "The King Is Coming," his visits to our tiny venues decreased. Yet even though we didn't see him very often and he was involved in a completely different kind of Christian music, he hadn't forgotten us.

By the seventies Bill Gaither was the contemporary Christian music scene's guiding force. Even though many southern gospel groups, such as the Speers, recorded his material, Bill was never seen as a quartet or southern gospel man. His music was aimed at a younger, hipper audience than those who followed the Blackwoods and Statesmen. So while the Imperials might have topped the charts with "He Touched Me," the performers who usually recorded Bill's songs represented a new audience that was tuned in to "Jesus" music. Southern gospel music appealed to grandparents and parents while Gaither appealed to the college crowd.

As we watched Bill quickly become a mega-star, we didn't realize he was still watching us too. Though his trio was drawing audiences of ten thousand when we were lucky to draw a few hundred, he was keeping track of our every move. It seemed that he had a plan and we were a part of it. It took awhile for Bill's plan to hatch, but by the mid seventies, Bill contacted us. We were shocked to find out that the famous songwriter and performer not only wanted to produce our future records for Word, but he wanted us to sing at his world-famous Praise Gathering in Indianapolis.

Getting a chance to work with Bill in the studio was great and not completely unexpected, but the opportunity to perform at Praise Gathering was something that we never would have anticipated. Essentially it is an annual three-day celebration of contemporary Christian music. Each year this event draws more than eleven thousand people who purchase tickets a year in advance just to be a part of what can only be described as a "worship" experience. Not only were we honored to be the first southern gospel group to perform there, we were thrilled just to have an opportunity to listen to the huge array of new songs and singers that were having such a positive effect on the nation's youth.

After we arrived in Indianapolis and set up, we took in the sounds and rubbed elbows with not only performers, but fans too. I felt like a teenager again. One just couldn't help but get excited about the place and the people. It seemed to me that this gathering was a new version of the old-fashioned singing conventions that Glen and I had loved when we were younger. I was amazed that Bill could bring together so much talent in one place. Over the years I would come to discover that Bill has a special knack for bringing people together.

After a while, the excitement I felt from this "young" environment turned to apprehension. As I tuned in to Amy Grant and watched this Tennessee teen become one with the audience, I began to question what people would think of us. Bill had never invited a southern gospel group before. This audience didn't turn out for our all-night singings, buy our records, or watch shows like the *Jubilee*. Most of them had never seen a shaped note or heard of the Blackwoods or the Goodmans. Most would have thought the Stamps were something found at a post office. I began to wonder if Bill knew what he was doing putting us in front of this crowd.

As I was about to walk onstage, I was still questioning what these "big-church" folks and kids were going to do when we began our piano-driven four-part harmonies. I could picture them strolling out to take a break during our segment, or worse, staying in their seats and laughing at our "old-fashioned" style. Yet we had promised Bill we would go on, our name was on the program, and there would be no backing out. Just before we walked out, something calmed my fears. Together the five of us prayed that God would open a tiny door of acceptance for the Cathedrals so that at least one person would be moved by our music.

At first it seemed as though my worse fears were going to come true. As we began singing, many in the crowd looked at us as though we had just arrived from another planet. Thousands appeared to be wondering what in the world was going on. Yet they didn't leave, didn't laugh, and didn't ignore us. They remained in their seats and gave us a chance to show our talents, spirit, and musical style. And one by one, song by song, they seemed to come over to our side. By the end of the first set, we found ourselves deluged with "amens" and standing ovations. Many of the kids in that audience must have thought we had invented a new kind of music. They had never heard southern gospel, but they were relating to it. They couldn't stay still. Music directors from huge churches and college-age "Jesus-freaks" were urging us on too. We had awakened long-forgotten memories of dinners on the ground and church with Grandma. I looked over at the other guys and realized that they too knew they were part of something special. Dripping in sweat, throats throbbing, and knees weak, we left the stage with more energy than when we had started.

That day at the Praise Gathering was a turning point. I still don't know why Bill Gaither chose us to break in southern gospel there at that time, but we will never be able to thank him enough for shining a bright light on what we were doing.

The high we felt as we left that Indiana stage was made even more pronounced when we got word that within days of our appearance at Praise Gathering, our booker's office was flooded with calls from churches who had sent representatives to the Gaithers' big event. These inquiries were from people who had never been interested in southern gospel in the past but couldn't wait to introduce us to their flocks. To me this seemed an absolute miracle. One week the people who tried to sell us couldn't give us away to people who wanted a southern gospel quartet, and the next week we had three and four offers for the same date to work in places where people had barely even heard of southern gospel music. As we traveled down the road to those first few dates, I was beginning to feel as though the Lord had a plan for us after all. Judging from the fact that Glen was sleeping better and spending less time fretting over the books, I think he was feeling the same.

The next important step for us was to gain success in the recording field. We had put out scores of what we had thought were great singles and albums, but they had been largely ignored. Then we released a special song called "Last Sunday," and radio stations finally began to play Cathedral music.

In the South as well as in the Midwest, we were now playing before larger and more enthusiastic crowds each month. These people not only knew who we were, but they were buying our records and staying after the shows to get to know us. What a difference this made in our lives! By 1977 all five of us could not only pay our bills and have enough money left over for an occasional evening out with our families, but we also were seeing visible signs that the message of our music was hitting home.

One night in a church in Indiana, we held an altar call, and as was now usual, several came forward to give their lives to Christ. On this evening, from separate sides of the church, a man and a woman independently stepped to the platform to pray. Through a miracle not of our making, God's Word had been heard through our music and had moved these two to rededicate their lives to him. As they got up off their knees and turned, the man and woman saw each other, stopped for a moment, and then smiled. We didn't know it until much later, but this man and woman had been scheduled for divorce court the next day. They had given up on their marriage and each other. Thanks to an altar call, that meeting with a judge was canceled and these two were brought together again to be one with the Lord and with each other. They still come to see us perform and are now one of their church's strongest guiding couples.

Stories like this one played out night after night. We repeatedly were told that the Cathedrals' music was bringing people home and giving them hope. In 1977 we journeyed to Nashville for Gospel Music Week. As Glen and I sat with our wives in the audience for the Dove Awards, we expected nothing. Yet four times that night they called our names. We won for song, album, single, and group. We were thrilled, moved to tears, and humbled all at the same time. As our many friends gathered around to pat us on the back, give us a hug, or shake our hands, Glen and I sought out our wives. These awards were theirs not ours. It was Clara and Van who had supported us when no one else cared. It was these two incredible women who had prayed for us each night. They had kept the faith and held us and our families together during the long, hard times. They had shouldered a much tougher burden at home than we had ever shouldered on the road. Glen and I knew these two women were God's most precious gifts to us. Far more than us, they deserved the good things now happening in our lives.

After the Dove Awards, Glen and I experienced the highest moments in our careers. Each place where we played welcomed us with open arms, and fans now stayed in their seats for every song. What a joy it was to be successful doing something we loved to do! This joy was made all the sweeter by our years of having gone through the storms of doubt and despair.

With God's help, we had managed to climb out of a deep hole and were now rubbing elbows with the top names in the business. Thanks to people like Les Beasley, W. B. Nowlin, and Bill Gaither, audiences were clamoring for us in cities and towns all across the United States and Canada. Unlike Moses, we hadn't wandered through the wilderness for years and then not been allowed to cross over to the Promised Land. We had made it, and the view was great!

At that point in my life, I couldn't see anything but cloudless days ahead. I thought the tests were over and that I would always be living in the land of milk and honey. I didn't know that just over the horizon a storm was brewing.

{ *chapter twenty* }

STARTING
ALL OVER AGAIN

W HEN VAN AND I went to Cincinnati to work on our latest recording project, I was on top of the world. For the first time since we had left Rex Humbard, everyone wanted the Cathedrals. After a decade of working night and day just to scrape by, life had suddenly gotten so much easier. Things were so great that I couldn't foresee a single problem that would take more than a few minutes to solve.

Van went shopping while I went about working out the details for our next album release. Caught up in the moment, I barely noted something I overheard. The statement seemed so farfetched that I all but laughed it off as a joke. Yet that unfunny joke worked on me, and because it wasn't the first day of April, I decided to make a few calls to put the rumor to bed. When I got off the phone I was closer to crying than laughing, and I barely had the strength to return the receiver to the hook. What I had thought was a bad attempt at a joke was instead the cold, cruel truth.

By the time I found Van and began to tell her what had happened, anger was surging through my body like electricity. When I had finished explaining it all to my wife, I was close to a boiling rage. I was hurt and mad at the same time.

It seemed that some months before, a well-known promoter had gone to the other three members of our group and convinced them that the time was right for them to move on, form their own quartet, and leave the "old men" behind. The individual who sold our three partners on this concept thought that George and I were holding back the talented young blood. This expert felt sure that George

Amon, Mack, and Lorne could fly much higher without us in the southern gospel skies. Without my knowledge, they had put together everything they needed to make the move.

I may have been in the dark about the move, but I was not an ignorant man. I knew the business as well as I knew anything. At some point I had fully expected the guys to move on. What I hadn't counted on was for them to all move at once. Now that we had lost three-fifths of the group in one swoop, it seemed as if the Cathedrals had been blown completely out of the water. For a few moments, I couldn't see how George and I could keep going. It was as if a thief had come in the night and stolen everything we had.

Van could sense that I had been badly shaken, but as I looked into her eyes, I didn't see panic, pain, or anger. Remarkably she seemed calm and assured.

"Glen," she said quietly, "we have to pray about this."

I am a bit ashamed now that the first thing I thought of was not getting on my knees and asking God for help. I had too quickly become caught up in self-pity and anger to even consider turning the problem over to the Lord. Now, with seemingly no other recourse, I bowed my head and asked for guidance and strength. Almost immediately my head began to clear and my feet found their way back to solid ground.

I thought about calling George right then, but I didn't really want to tell him the bad news over the phone. Forgetting the work I should have been doing on the record, Van and I hurried home.

As soon as I walked through the door, George sensed that I had bad news. From the look on my face, he probably assumed that someone had died. While the Cathedrals hadn't expired, I hated to tell him we were on life support and the clock was ticking.

As I figured, George was as blown away by the news as I had been. I can still hear him asking, "Are you sure?" After a few moments of quiet thought, he looked back at me, his eyes moist, his strong, deep voice unsteady and wavering.

"Maybe this is the Lord's way of telling us to hang it up," he said.

I wondered the same thing. Perhaps God was telling us to pull back and leave things to people who were younger and stronger. Yet as hard as I tried to convince myself that this was the way God wanted it, I couldn't. The only person who really thought us too old to praise our Savior was the promoter who had sold our friends on the idea.

George had been stunned to think that someone considered him to old to hold up his end of the work load. Yet he understood why the guys had made this move. They were young, ambitious, and felt as if they needed to try their wings in new skies. As George reminded me, he had done the same thing early in his career. Still, we had to figure out what we should do next.

Finally, we decided to include God in the discussion. We both bowed our heads and gave our problems to him. After that prayer we still had doubts, fears, and a bit of anger, but we now both felt confident that we needed to try to rebuild the quartet. We didn't have much of a plan, but at least we were together in our desires. We weren't going to give up without a fight.

"Glen," George said as we parted company, "let's give it our best shot, and if we can't pull it together, we will know the Lord wants us to settle down and find something else to do."

Still, I couldn't sleep that night for thinking about the monumental task ahead. I questioned whether the promoters, bookers, and fans would consider our new group the real Cathedrals or whether they would flock to the group with the other three guys. And what about the label? Would they keep us on board or drop us?

I could envision everything George and I had worked for crumbling in front of us. Losing the Cathedrals would be like losing a child. I didn't know if I would ever get over it.

The next day the sun came up as usual. I picked up the phone and began to call those who had booked the Cathedrals for their churches or venues. We were no longer the quartet they had signed. Having just two members probably didn't even qualify us to be considered a group. I fully expected those who had begged for us a few weeks earlier to cancel our appearances. Yet rather than slam the door on me, nearly all of them told me to find a piano player and come. Most of them said that just having George and me would be enough. They didn't even ask us to cut our price. I was in shock!

George was as moved and thrilled as I was that people out in the real world seemed to believe we weren't too old to draw. One man even told us, "Glen Payne and George Younce *are* the Cathedrals. So you all come ahead and be ready for a long show!"

With the good news that we were still wanted as a starting point, we worked our way past wondering if we should go on and moved into the stage of finding a couple of guys to fill our holes. We came up with a short list and got back on the phone.

One young man on our list had been singing with the Hoppers. George and I both felt that Kirk Talley had a very commercial sound that would blend well with ours. We prayed he would be willing to take a chance on our being able to put things back together. We contacted Kirk, met with him in Jackson, Mississippi, and hired him before he finished the first song.

Then we were fortunate to find Steve Lee, who not only sang baritone, but played piano. With Kirk and Steve signed up, we hurriedly worked out some simple arrangements and hit the road.

We didn't know what to expect from our fans, but when Kirk started to sing "I Know a Man," he blew the house away. I could almost read the lips of people whispering to one another, "Yeah, they're the Cathedrals! This is the real thing!"

For the first time in his life, even George was speechless. When Kirk finished, George nodded, threw up his hands, and said, "Wow." At that point all doubts about who the real Cathedrals were washed out of our minds.

Besides the fans and the bookers, another person who hadn't lost faith in us was Bill Gaither. With him behind us, the label wasn't going to cut us loose either. In the studio Bill provided us with incredible material and wonderful arrangements. When we finished recording our *Stepping in the Water* album, I thought it was the best thing I had worked on since *In the Garden* with the Weatherfords. As it turned out, gospel music fans and radio stations thought so too. The single "Stepping in the Water" stayed number one for ten months in a row! The hard times I had anticipated were simply not going to happen.

As the seventies wound down, we were really getting wound up. I was feeling so good about the way things were going that I had all but forgotten the anger and doubt that had clouded my mind a few months earlier. Each day I thanked the Lord for his gifts and never did I feel moved to ask him for anything else. Yet as I was about to discover, he wasn't done giving good things to us.

One night in Arkansas, when George and I were on the bus discussing some business, Kirk and Steve had wandered out to hear a local gospel act perform. Just minutes before we were to go on, they rushed onto the bus and excitedly exclaimed, "We found us a piano player. This guy is incredible!"

George and I both knew how young, inexperienced guys could get worked up over people who in the light of day were pretty normal. Besides, we didn't think we needed a fifth member in the group at this time. But Kirk and Steve wouldn't let it rest. Finally, sensing that we wouldn't get any peace until we jumped out and heard this miracle man, the two of us walked backstage. Within minutes the piano licks of Roger Bennett had blown away us wily, old veterans too!

But I had reservations. Roger didn't even look old enough to take driver's education, let alone join a touring quartet. Kirk assured me, however, that Roger was not only out of high school, he was in college.

As talented as Roger was, I urged him to finish his college work and then get back to us. Roger didn't want to do that. He hailed from a family from Strawberry, Arkansas, who had haunted singing conventions and gospel concerts for years. It had always been his dream to play for a top gospel group. Being the pianist for the Cathedrals was far more important to him than anything else.

I told Roger that he had to work things out with his parents before I would even consider letting him join the Cathedrals. I felt kind of silly asking a college kid for a "note" from his parents, but I did it anyway. To my surprise, his parents not only let him go, they urged him to quit college and give music a shot. At that point I had no choice but to give the boy a bunk on the bus.

I had worked with some green kids in my life, but Roger took the cake. His knees and arms were like jelly his first few nights with us. He could barely say, "Hi." Every time George would call out his name, he would freeze like a deer locked in a car's headlights. Yet when he sat down at the keyboard, he performed magic. Within a couple of weeks he was as solid as anyone I had seen in a long time.

It quickly became apparent that Roger was a godsend, because just after we got comfortable with him, Steve Lee decided that he simply wasn't cut out for life on the road. I understood that it took a special kind of mentality to put up with one one-night stand after another. This life wasn't like the real world, and to work in this field you had to sacrifice a great deal. For Steve the price was not worth it. Though I hated to see him go, I wouldn't have wanted him to stay if he wasn't happy. He had to be where God wanted him.

By now a change in personnel didn't scare me as much as it had a year before. As a matter of fact, George and I were pretty blasé about it. We figured that when one door closed another would open. Our faith was rewarded when we found Mark Trammell on the other side of the door.

Mark had worked with Kirk in the past and had been singing with the Kingsmen. A solid baritone, Mark was a fine person whose style not only worked with our sound, but actually enhanced it in a manner we had never before known. He made us better. Mark was also the perfect quartet man offstage too. He would watch George and me do something once, and the next time he would do it. I suddenly found him loading equipment that I had always loaded in the past. He rolled up cable, sold product, and even cleaned up the bus. Every day he would do something else to make George's and my jobs easier.

In many ways we had become better than ever. Our sound was smooth and full, and Kirk, Roger, and Mark all sang solos as fine and Spirit-filled as anything we had ever done. All of them felt that being part of the Cathedrals was a gift from God. And maybe it was because of the group's overall attitude, but at every turn the Lord was blessing us. We were pulling down awards, playing dates in places where quartets never worked, and even showing up on television shows once reserved for country or pop acts. After a few months of working with this crew, I began to believe that we were even getting close to living up to the lofty billing Howard Goodman always gave us.

Special songs were coming our way like never before. Miss Isabell, an Arkansas songwriter, sent us something that sounded as if Marty Robbins should have been cutting it. It was a Spanish/western-style ballad called "Mexico." She had given it to us because she thought we weren't afraid to take chances with our music. We took a chance with "Mexico," and gospel music fans loved it even though many believed this unusual song would flop.

Roger brought us an Ann Ballard composition entitled "Roll Away Trouble River." It wasn't a song cut from the convention school mold, but it carried a hope- and Christ-filled message. This too was a song that others might have passed on, but it became a strong single for us.

Dian Wilkerson wrote "We Shall See Jesus" just for the Cathedrals. This powerful songwriter had sent us more than twenty different songs that we had rejected before we finally received this one. With this gift, Dian presented us not only with one of our signature songs, but with the reminder that we should never quit trying to do what we feel the Lord calling us to do. Persistence pays off.

Mark Taunton, our old buddy who had left us to found his own group, came back to us with something he had written especially for the Cathedrals' new sound. "Sunshine and Roses" not only helped us win a number of important awards, but it touched thousands of hearts and rebuilt a bridge between George and me and our old friend and partner.

Everywhere we looked Christ was making something special happen in our lives. Each day we were grateful for the new men we had hired. It seemed that the energy of their youth had revitalized both George and me. Rather than going along on a comfortable path, Roger, Kirk, and Mark had pushed us to try new things. Without the influence of this young blood, we may not have cut some of our contemporary-sounding records. The creativity and joy these guys added to us constantly reminded me that the booker who had said that "George and I *were* the Cathedrals" was wrong. The Cathedrals were a team, and each member was as important as the next.

George had once told me that he and I were a whole lot like Moses. We had wandered lost and confused for a long while, paid a few dues, and suffered a few trials, but that was where the comparison ended. Unlike Moses, God had let us walk in the promised land.

One night George glanced over at me after a show and said, "Old man, you made it." Just a few years earlier the thought of anyone calling me old scared me. The word *old* reminded me of how I had felt when our three young partners moved on leaving us in the lurch. I had even believed that our fans didn't want this "old man" anymore. But now I felt so young, alive, and energized that George could call me old whenever he wanted. During the last two years I had discovered that old was just a state of mind, and with our current tour schedule, it was about the only state where we weren't being booked. Yes, I really was living in the promised land.

chapter twenty-one

SHOWERS
OF BLESSINGS

Bᴙ ᴛʜᴇ ᴇᴀʀʟʏ ᴇɪɢʜᴛɪᴇꜱ I was having so much fun being the bass singer for the Cathedral Quartet that I thought I might just get arrested. It should have been illegal to be this happy and fulfilled. Whether I was performing on stage, traveling on the bus, talking with fans, or spending time with my family, I had all the energy in the world. People wondered if I had uncovered the fountain of youth. Every time I looked around, more good things were happening. Once again my life was filled with unclouded days and untroubled waters.

With good news piled on top of good news, with record sales at their highest point ever, and with more and more requests from major bookers for our shows, it was so easy to feel good about everything. The most rewarding facet of our work, however, was not counting sales receipts or watching our records climb the charts, it was going back to full houses in places that used to ignore us. Everyone wants to be accepted and liked, and now we were experiencing those feelings everywhere we went. Our rise in popularity was opening a host of other doors as well.

Billy Graham asked us to appear with him during some of his crusades. Singing in front of fifty thousand people hungry to hear the gospel was a wonderful opportunity and one of the most profound experiences of my life. Who would have thought that a couple of high school dropouts from the cotton fields of Texas and the woods of Carolina would ever be lifted so high? Wow! Ain't God good?

Glen, Kirk, Roger, and Mark were not just my teammates and best friends, they were my role models. As I watched the Lord use our music to bring thousands closer to him, I fell to my knees each night happy and honored to have these four beside me. Nevertheless, I knew we couldn't keep this group together forever. I was experienced enough to realize that eventually the young guys would want to move on. Yet locked in the bliss of having a quartet that seemed to always hit the right notes and find the best blend, I tried to ignore this possibility. Ignoring it, however, did not keep it from happening.

Kirk Talley was like a son to Glen and me, and when he came to us expressing his desire to start a family group with his brother and sister-in-law, we were not going to stand in his way. I had long felt that there were no harmonies as rich and pure as those created by a blend of family voices. In my mind the sound the Talleys were going to fashion had the potential to be one of the sweetest ever known in inspirational music. Best of all, we were able to give Kirk our blessing and keep him around too—for almost two years the Talleys toured with the Cathedrals.

We knew that it wasn't going to be easy to find someone to take Kirk's place. Our fans loved him, and anyone who followed him was going to be judged by a mighty high standard. After quite a bit of searching, we finally found our new tenor performing with the Singing Americans. Danny Funderburk and his vocal group were working part time in gospel music, and he wanted to get involved with a quartet that was singing almost every night. Though it took him a little while to find his step within our arrangements, he won over our fans his first night onstage. Danny was an outgoing young man who couldn't wait to talk to people, hug their necks, and tell them how much he appreciated them coming out to see the Cathedrals. He was the best public relations man we ever had. Above all else, Danny was sincere. After only six months he was one of the most popular people in the quartet field and had hit his full musical stride too. At every performance people were asking, "Where did they find this guy?"

Then it came time to say good-bye to someone else. After several years on the piano, Roger Bennett received an offer to help begin a record company. For the young man from Strawberry, Arkansas, it was an opportunity just too good to refuse. I had seen Roger grow from a frightened kid to one of the most talented all-around performers I had ever known. The only part he couldn't sing well was bass—which relieved me a bit. He could play anything on the piano, he could spot a great new composition, and he was a tremendous arranger. As I hugged Roger good-bye, I couldn't imagine ever finding anyone who could compete with him.

God sent us a young man whose skills were honed in different areas. Not only was Gerald Wolfe a great pianist and wonderful Christian man, but he knew how to use an arrangement to lift the music to a higher level. With his diverse musical experiences and dedicated spirit, he helped us refine our sound and challenged us to continue to grow as artists. Once again I discovered that new blood not only challenged us mentally, but spiritually as well. Rather than sitting back and coasting, enjoying our successful days, Glen and I were being forced to become deeper both spiritually and musically.

Our professional growth paid off not only in bookings in the United States and Canada, but across the Atlantic Ocean as well. We received an opportunity no gospel quartet had ever been given: We were invited to travel to the United Kingdom. Imagine singing southern gospel music in England! Better yet, we were invited to sing with the world-famous London Philharmonic Orchestra.

It goes without saying that we were overwhelmed that this prestigious group would want to share a stage with us. We were even more overwhelmed when during rehearsals we heard their arrangements of our songs. The whole thing just blew me away. I had never even thought about what it would be like to hear classically trained musicians playing gospel music, but as I would discover, it was something special! The orchestra's sound was so rich, full, and perfect that it caused chills to run up and down my spine even before I got a chance to add my part. I will never find adequate words to fully describe it. It was a rapturous experience.

From the first time we rehearsed until we finally went onstage for our scheduled performance, I didn't come down from my spiritual high. When we began to sing that night, I felt as if I were visiting with the saints. God had to have been paying particular attention that evening, because each of us was *on* like we had never been *on* before. After a few songs, I became so involved with the audience that I forgot where I was and who was backing us up. I was just being swept up by the same Spirit I had felt when I first heard God calling out to me as a child in our small family church. It was like being saved all over again. I wanted to cry, laugh, shout, and sing—and over the course of that hour, I did do all of those things.

That evening we ended our performance with one of our favorite songs, "God Himself a Lamb." The audience had been very enthusiastic all evening but now had fallen into a quiet, worshipful attitude. When we ended the final note, things remained hushed for a moment, and then, one by one, people began to stand up. Soon the entire crowd had made it to their feet and were clapping wildly. Their applause was deafening. What I hadn't realized was that the orchestra had risen too. I later learned that we were the first act in more than a dozen years to be given a standing ovation by the London Philharmonic. While I believe the Cathedrals are not deserving of such praise, I know the Lord is. I am sure the standing ovation was caused not by our music, but by his Spirit overwhelming everyone in the place just as he had overwhelmed me.

My mom and dad always said that if you do your work in God's service and for his honor, every day you will be lifted up and blessed in some manner. I believe this to be true, yet all of us have special moments when it seems as if we are completely engulfed in the Spirit unlike at any other time in our lives. For me one of those moments was that night in London; another happened much closer home.

We had been to New York City on many occasions, often playing in large churches in Brooklyn, Queens, and the Bronx. Now we were invited back to the Big Apple not to sing in a church, but to perform at Radio City Music Hall. All my life I had heard of Radio City. I had even driven past it, gawking like a tourist. Many of the shows I had listened to on the radio during my youth had originated from there, and the entertainers who worked this stage were some of the most famous in the world. For a performer this venue was like no other. Radio City had always been off limits for gospel quartets.

The popularity of southern gospel music and inspirational music in general had no doubt triggered Radio City's experiment, placing religious music center stage in New York. At least that is what I figured when they asked the Cathedrals to be a part of the bill there. But as we signed our names to the contract, Glen and I decided not to analyze what it was that had brought us here; we were just going to revel in seeing our name in lights on the big marquee and enjoy the fact that we were getting to sing our Spirit-filled music on the old stage. This represented quite a jump for a group who once hoped to interest an audience enough to stay in an auditorium after the Happy Goodmans had left the stage and we still had to do our portion of the program.

Joining us on that stage was one of the world's finest gospel music ensembles. The honor we felt in working with the Brooklyn Tabernacle Choir was unlike any we had ever known, with the possible exception of our date with the London Philharmonic. If you weren't moved to shout "Amen!" after hearing that choir sing, you were either dead or mute!

For two straight evenings Radio City sold out every seat for our performance. I couldn't believe that city people were willing to pay twenty dollars a seat to hear southern gospel music and a local choir. Not only did they buy every ticket, they practically jumped out of their seats when Glen hit his high notes. As they gave him a standing ovation, I couldn't help but say, "Well, the old man finally woke up! Don't you just love old people?" Evidently New Yorkers sure did.

Once we had felt unworthy of the exposure we had been given on *The Gospel Music Jubilee*. Now we were blazing trails by appearing on NBC's *Today Show*. I was again overwhelmed. All we had ever wanted was to sing gospel music, and now Glen and I were applying for senior citizen's discounts at the same time we were being considered "cool" by many in music's youth-oriented mainstream.

Even with all the success we were enjoying, we had to deal with the revolving door of gospel music. It seemed like I had just gotten to know Gerald Wolfe when he left us to go to work in his own ministry. I hated to see him go, but this time we didn't have to look far to find a replacement. Roger Bennett had grown tired of the studio and wanted to get back in front of an audience. We were more than happy to welcome him back to the Cathedrals. With Roger on the keyboard, we didn't miss a beat.

By 1987 we didn't have enough days in the year for all the booking requests we were receiving. No longer were we gospel music's stepchildren; we were fully accepted along with the Stamps, Goodmans,

Speers, and all the other top names. Just knowing this should have made me feel like I could conquer the whole world. Yet while my spirit was willing, my flesh suddenly seemed weak!

In September I really began to feel my age. My arm and shoulder started to ache from time to time; it was getting harder for me to catch my breath after each song; and I no longer had the bounce in my step that had characterized me since I was a toddler, dancing for nickels at the cotton mill store. If I kept falling apart like this, I feared Glen would soon be calling *me* the "old man." That was something I just couldn't bear. Though three years my senior, he now seemed much younger onstage and off.

One evening, in the middle of an early fall tour in Denver, I decided that a walk up the motel stairs might make me feel better. I needed something to restore my vitality and thought that exercise might just do the trick. Yet five steps up I felt the aches and pains flying at me with a renewed determination. My body wasn't just complaining, it was shouting at me to stop! By the time I had climbed just one flight of stairs I was dizzy, sweating, and so tired I had to sit down. After resting a few minutes, I walked up another flight then again stopped and sat down. It took me almost ten minutes to make it to my room on the third floor.

All I could think of was unlocking my door, hanging out the "Do Not Disturb" sign, putting on the night latch, and going to bed. I just wanted the pulsing pain that forced me to take breaths in short gulps to stop. Yet rather than ease up, it grew worse. Finally, when the shooting bursts ran through my body and forced me to moan, I dragged myself up and struggled to the door of an empty room. I managed to open it just before I collapsed.

No one was in the hallway to hear my cries for help, so I realized that I had to make it to the phone. Yet it was twelve feet away and I couldn't even stand up. On my belly I began the longest trip I had ever known. Inch by inch I pulled myself forward. Sweat drenched my body and my heart felt like it would explode. How I wanted to give up and just go to sleep. My brain screamed out for rest, but I knew that if I quit crawling, I would die alone in a strange hotel room and not be able to say good-bye to all who had meant so much to my life. My face to the carpet, I vowed I wasn't going to do that. I didn't mind so much cashing it in and leaving this old world for Glory. After all, my life had been rich and full, much more than I deserved, and my Savior was waiting for me on the other side. But I wasn't going to let myself die until I had a chance to tell my wife and kids I loved them, the guys in the group how much it meant for me to sing with them, and old Glen Payne how much I appreciated his always having faith in me.

Finally I got to the nightstand and pulled the phone down on the floor. With the last bit of energy I could muster, I dialed Mark's room. After that I lost track of everything as the world became little more than an out-of-focus image of people rushing in and out, trying to pull me back from the grave. I was lying on the ground, but my mind was on Glory.

{ chapter twenty-two }

HOMECOMING

By THE TIME I heard the news about George, the ambulance had already taken him to the hospital. I knew that he had been experiencing pain and fatigue over the past few weeks, but I really didn't think it was anything serious; I just chalked it up to age. At the hospital, I barely recognized the old warrior. His voice was all but gone, his body was limp, and he was so very pale. For a second, I thought that I either had the wrong room or was staring at a dead man. But even as the shock registered on my face, a grin came to his. As ill as he was, he was trying to tell me that he was all right and not to worry.

The doctors informed us that George had suffered a severe heart attack. They now had him stabilized, but he couldn't get back on his feet until they put him through a battery of tests to discover the cause and extent of the damage. Even at this early hour, they indicated that the road to recovery was going to be a long one and that major surgery was going to be required.

My initial impulse was to cancel our next few performances and stay in Denver with my friend. At this point the Cathedrals just didn't seem to be too important. George, however, being the quartet man that he was, would have none of it. He ordered me to get on the bus and make the next booking. It was the hardest thing I had done since leaving my father's hospital bed to join the Weatherfords.

Until then I hadn't thought much about what life would be like without George. I had just assumed that he and I would always be together with the Cathedrals. I had not even considered the group without him. Now I was forced to contemplate performing without George at my side and maybe even living a life void of his friendship and support. I didn't know if I could do it.

That first night we set aside a mike for George and explained to the crowd what had happened and told them that they were not going to get to hear the world's best bass singer. I wanted each person in attendance to know that the empty mike represented the Cathedral who was there in spirit. Then, to emphasize just how much he meant to us, I said something that sounded a bit impulsive and rash. "No one will fill this spot until George Younce comes back to us."

Most people in gospel music didn't really believe me. More than forty years earlier the Blackwoods had lost several family members in a plane crash, and they had replaced them and moved on. Even the Stamps had moved on when V. O. had died. Nevertheless, my feelings were firm. George had been the Cathedrals' only bass singer and had made us a quartet back when we had been just a trio. We simply would not function as a trio again.

Somehow we got through that first show and the ones that followed. Every night the empty mike served as a reminder to us and our fans that we were going to lift our friend up to God with each song and each prayer.

For ten days, George lay in Denver's Porter Memorial Hospital. With his wife and brother at his side, he fought to gain enough strength to return home to Ohio. When he was finally released, it was to the loving care of Clara. She was told to keep him quiet and rested. The former was not very hard, because for the first time in his life, George didn't have much to say. Both of his lungs had collapsed during the attack, and all he could manage was a hoarse whisper.

Whenever our tours brought us home, I headed off to check on George. The more I visited with my friend, the more I questioned whether he would ever rejoin the Cathedrals. What worried me even more was wondering how much longer we would have him period. At times I felt as though I were looking at a dying man.

My father had recently passed away, and I was trying to imagine Christmas without him. Dad had lived a long life and had experienced a full range of joy and happiness. His death had been difficult, but it seemed to fit in with the natural order of things. George, on the other hand, was only fifty-seven. He was too young with too much left to give to be at death's door. I knew I could manage Christmas without Dad, but I had to have George there.

Meanwhile, I still had to go on stage night after night. It was extremely hard to fill in as master of ceremonies, tell jokes, and try to come up with witty ways to respond to the crowd when I was so worried about George. It was getting tough to work with that empty microphone standing on my left.

As fall gave way to the first hint of winter, I began to receive calls from guys who were interested in trying out for our "open" bass spot. This made me extremely angry. They were treating George as if he were finished, but I wasn't ready to concede that until George told me he was through. I still felt that we had a bass singer, and I didn't want to do anything, even on a temporary basis, that would make it appear that we were writing George off. Yet as he was wheeled into surgery the day before Thanksgiving, I had my doubts.

George came home on December 7, and he had even less voice than before the operation. "What will be, will be what the Lord wants it to be," he kept repeating. I think that is why when we would pray together he never asked for his voice back, but just for strength to accept the next role the Lord wanted him to play.

George began to spend his days working on the same voice training exercises he had learned forty years earlier at the Stamps-Baxter Singing School. Clara was almost amused at some of his first efforts. I don't know what the neighbors thought, but after only a few days, he was as good as most bass singers in modest church choirs. At least he would still be able to enjoy music to some degree. Because he had so far to go, I was shocked when less than a week later George told me he wanted to fill up that empty mike again. I issued a press release stating that George would be back with us as a vocalist when we opened our tour in Stuart, Florida, but still I wondered just how he would be able to do it.

We carefully planned our transformation back to a real quartet. Instead of our "normal" show, we picked out songs that would allow George to sing without having to push too hard. The last thing I wanted was for the fans and media to realize just how weak he still was. I didn't want to expose them to anything less than a perfect George Younce.

Before we went on stage, George came up to me. I could tell he had something important on his mind. I wondered whether he now felt he was trying to come back too soon. That was the last thing on his mind.

"Glen," George almost whispered, "I am changing the show a bit. I want to kick things off with 'Plan of Salvation.'"

I was stunned.

"We really don't want to do that," I quickly told him. I hoped he hadn't been able to read the shock on my face. "I mean . . . what if your voice breaks up and . . ."

George knew that I was trying to protect him, but he would have none of it. With a wave of his hand, he stopped me from finishing my thought.

"I just got through talking to God," George explained. "I told him that if he wanted me to keep singing, then I was going to be the best I could be. I wasn't going to go halfway. So this is where I find out what he wants. If I fall on my face, then it will be time to hang it up. I can deal with that."

I had known my friend long enough not to argue with him, yet I still didn't feel that it was a smart thing to do. I wanted him to wait a few weeks, get his confidence and his voice back, then when we all felt he was ready, really challenge himself. I certainly didn't want him going for broke right out of the blocks. But if that is what he thought the Lord wanted, then who was I to try to talk him out of it?

As we walked out that evening, we were all praying like mad, asking the Lord to give George the strength to meet his own expectations. As I looked out over the audience and saw the thousands who had been waiting to hear the Cathedral Quartet again, I sensed that they were praying too. When I glanced over at George, he looked scared but somehow at peace.

Before I was even ready for it, "Plan of Salvation" kicked things off. Jumping in, we all hit our parts for a verse and a chorus. Then it came time for Mark, Danny, and me to step back and let George try the bass solo. I'm sure we were more nervous than he was. With fans from all over the country, many of whom had driven hundreds of miles just to be with us, and Gordon Stoker, tenor singer for the Jordanaires, sitting in the front row mouthing the words, George took off. Miraculously, the sound that came from his throat was clear, smooth, and deep. As if by magic, we had the old George back with us.

I had a tough time making it through the rest of that song. My eyes were filled with tears and I felt a huge knot in my stomach. Mine was the weak voice; my throat was so tight that I could barely push out the words. In other words, I had never felt better! My heart was jumping for joy because a million prayers had been answered and the Cathedrals were again a quartet.

It took George just a few weeks to regain his full strength. By the time he could hit all of his notes on stage, he was hitting all of his jokes too. Like a small child, he was dancing, laughing, and having a good time. Life was sweeter now that he had come so close to losing what he had cherished so much. Life was more precious for me too, now that I had my partner back.

Ironically, even as we put the quartet back together, we were making changes. Danny felt a need to move on and become a soloist. With his incredible voice, I thought he needed to try to fly on his own. Replacing a member of the group was something I didn't relish, but before I could start fretting, God dropped someone on our doorstep.

I had known Ernie Hasse since he had been in junior high. Whenever we would perform near his hometown of Evansville, Indiana, he would not just come and listen, but stay and visit as we packed up. Tall, good-looking, a college graduate with a solid tenor voice, Ernie had been soloing when we ran into him again. I hadn't a clue that he was interested in becoming a part of our group, but when the possibility came up, Ernie jumped at the chance.

Even though we knew Ernie had the enthusiasm, George and I weren't sure he had the experience to fill Danny's spot. Nevertheless, we decided to try him out at a few engagements. When Ernie sang "Oh What a Savior," we knew he would be with us for as long as he wanted. Every night for almost a decade, "Oh What a Savior" and Ernie Hasse have brought the house down.

Once again new blood put us in touch with a younger segment of the gospel music audience. Ernie wasn't satisfied simply bringing us new ideas, however; he wanted to become an important part of our lives as well. So not only did our new tenor try to load and unload equipment faster than anyone we had ever seen, but he also convinced George's daughter Lisa that he was the world's most eligible bachelor. Within six months of joining the Cathedrals, Ernie became George's son-in-law. I thought there was poetic justice in George having a tenor invade his family.

I was hoping we could hold onto Mark Trammel long enough to fully break Ernie in, but that wasn't the way it turned out. In 1990 Mark left to go with Greater Vision. Over our many years together, I had grown to love Mark about as much as one could love a working partner. He was not just a first-rate singer, but an incredible friend and quartet man. I don't know what I would have done if he hadn't helped me pick up the slack when George was sick.

I was at a loss about who to bring in as our new baritone. Thankfully, Ernie wasn't. He told us about a young man he had sung with at Oakland City College who was now singing with a group called The Sound. This guy was not just a great singer, he assured us, but a solid musician too. That was good, because we had been spoiled by Mark's bass guitar playing.

Scott Fowler may have been in Ernie's class at school, but he looked like he was fresh out of junior high when we met him. If we hired this baby-faced kid, George figured we would need to apply for a day-care license. Nevertheless, he was a Cathedral within a week.

As the Cathedrals closed in on our thirtieth year in gospel music and George and I crept up on fifty years of singing in quartets, I figured the Lord would want us to slow down a bit. But rather than easing off and cutting back, George and I were forced to push into even higher gear as we passed sixty. A lot of this need to speed up and do more was because of Bill and Gloria Gaither—they were the culprits.

Bill called and asked if we could join some old friends to sing a couple of songs for a project he had felt called to pursue. On the prescribed date, George and I gathered with Howard and Vestal Goodman, Jake Hess, Hovie Lister, J. D. Sumner, and about twenty other gospel music old-timers to sing "Where Could I Go But to the Lord?" That was all we were supposed to do. Bill had only wanted to get a bunch of veterans together to create a once-in-a-lifetime musical event with that one song. As it turned out, he accomplished a whole lot more.

Never in my life had I joined so many great gospel stars in one room with one goal. The enthusiasm we felt was so incredible, the memories of working together over the years were so strong, and the sense of being caught up in the Spirit so great that we couldn't quit singing after "Where Could I Go?" We just kept going and going and going. Someone would say, "Hey, do you remember this one?" and with the piano hitting the introduction, we would all begin to harmonize. For three or four hours we kept singing and Bill kept his camera rolling. Ultimately this historic event was edited down to one hour and released as a video. I was proud to have been a part of something so worshipful and memorable. It was a day I would always treasure and one that I thought would never happen again.

I was surprised when a few months later Bill placed another call to George and me. He wanted to have the first "Homecoming" crowd reassemble to sing some more. This time he wanted us to be ready to sing all night.

A quartet man rarely gets a chance to harmonize in a choir, but that is what we have done ever since Bill began his "Homecoming" reunions. Comprised of the greatest gospel and contemporary Christian singers, this choir provides a worship experience for the performers as well as the audience.

We used to sing on the same bill with other gospel groups, but we were too busy rushing on and off the stage, packing and unpacking, to ever share a moment of prayer, much less a song. Now, thanks to what Bill and Gloria have done, George and I get to introduce the young guys in our group to the singers who gave us our big breaks, helped us during the bad times, and carved out a niche for our kind of music. In turn, Ernie, Roger, and Kirk introduce us to the up-and-comers in the business, and we get to "feel" what makes their new sounds so wonderful.

Over the past few years we have seen God continually work in our lives. Our piano player is just one example. Just three years ago Roger was diagnosed with cancer. We thought the quartet would lose him as a piano player, but we were even more concerned that his wife and family would lose him as a father and husband. Through faith and prayer combined with the finest in medical care, Roger not only didn't leave this world, he didn't leave us either. And each night he shares his testimony. I have watched him help thousands who were walking the same path of suffering. If you have followed the Cathedrals for very long, you know that we are living proof that God turns negatives into positives every day.

Over the course of the past ten years, the Cathedrals have enjoyed unimagined success. We have traveled to so many places that we are even working on wearing out our sixth bus! Not only have we been blessed by doing what we love, but we have been fulfilled by bringing the Great Commission to bring the Good News to so many people.

Our lives span the days from 78 rpm records to CDs, from radio to video, and from singing for a publishing company to having our own company. With my son-in-law, Bill Traylor, we have become business partners in the music industry through a company called Homeland. We have been able to provide a new recording label for artists who are where we were fifty years ago. So just as we are renewing old friendships with people through the Gaither Homecoming video series, we are meeting and helping new artists who will carry our music to the next generations.

The joys of growing old have been a blessing too. Daughter Carla and her husband, Bill, have given us two wonderful grandchildren, Jordan and Maria. As I write this, our son, Todd, and his wife, Lori, are just about to bring us another bundle of joy. And who could have asked for our youngest, Darla, to find a husband who is as special as Kevin? I thank God each day that he granted me these living blessings and examples of his wonder and power. As I watch George with his own grandchildren, I know he feels the same way.

The Bible says that God can do "immeasurably more than all we ask or imagine" (Ephesians 3:20). Certainly, even when I rushed home from the Texas cotton fields to catch the Stamps on the radio and fantasized about singing with them, I never dreamed dreams as big as those I have experienced.

A lot of people have made George's and my careers possible. We cannot acknowledge or thank them all even in the many words of this book, but we can go on living for the One for whom they live. We can go on singing of Christ and doing his will. We can go on lifting others to Jesus through our music. In doing so, we are acknowledging and thanking everyone of those who gave us a break, a prayer, a push, a prod, a song, a smile, a hug, a pledge of faith, and another chance. Each of those who have touched us is as much a member of the Cathedrals as we are. They are a part of God's wonderful harmony!